# The Complete Book of Floor Coverings

# The Complete Book of Floor Coverings

ROBERT Y. ELLIS

Charles Scribner's Sons
New York

Copyright © 1980 Charles Scribner's Sons

**Library of Congress Cataloging in Publication Data**

Ellis, Robert Y
   The complete book of floor coverings.

   Includes index.
   1. Floor coverings.    I. Title.
TH2525.E44    645'.1    79-53958
ISBN 0-684-16382-9

1 3 5 7 9 11 13 15 17 19   V/C   20 18 16 14 12 10 8 6 4 2

Printed in the United States of America

# Contents

# Introduction

This book is intended to serve you as a floor covering consumer and (if you wish) as a do-it-yourselfer by:

1. helping you figure out which type of floor covering would be most appropriate for your needs;

2. showing you how to install your floor covering or, at the very least, what you have a right to expect from the professional installer.

When it comes to buying floor covering the consumer often is at a loss. And, once he/she buys something, there can be the nagging possibility that the right decision has not been made. Indeed, there may be a sneaking suspicion that one has been "taken." This is because there are so many floor covering dealers offering all kinds of "deals" and because there are some 400 "mills" all claiming to sell the best floor covering. The consumer, therefore, is stuck in the middle of an almost incomprehensible morass of good and bad information.

And then there is the installation!

On a given day some men arrive at the home and start installing. For a few hours or a day they take over your home. They are usually a friendly enough lot who come in, move your furniture all over the place, put all sorts of interesting things all over your floor, finally spread out your carpet or linoleum, cut it to fit and fasten it down in some mysterious way, with all kinds of strange tools, move the furniture back, wave good-bye and leave. The average consumer hopes the job was done right and trusts that he/she dealt with a salesperson who will stand behind the sale and installation.

Or you may want to do it yourself. But, while you may have done carpentry or other jobs around the home perhaps you have never tackled floor covering. This to you is still a mystery. It is true that there are some aspects of floor covering installation which require somewhat sophisticated procedures and tools. But when you stop to consider the large number of installers there are in most neighborhoods, what it really takes to do the job, and the fact that many mills are aiming at the do-it-yourselfer with products developed especially for him, one realizes the time is ripe for a book of instructions written for the layman.

Indeed, the trade publication, *Floor Covering Weekly,* published a study recently which predicted that the do-it-yourself market will increase by leaps and bounds in the next decade. The intelligent, informed consumer and the do-it-yourselfer are here to stay and have been recognized by most manufacturers of household products. Their time now has come in the floor covering field.

This book, therefore, is dedicated to you, M./Ms. Consumer and/or Do-It-Yourselfer. You will find the first half (Chapters 1 through 5) devoted to learning how to buy intelligently—what product you should invest in and (perhaps most important) how much you need. The latter is covered in Chapter 1. Admittedly, figuring how many square feet or square yards of material are needed can be confusing, even for the pro. So don't get bogged down in Chapter 1. You may want to skip to Chapters 2 through 5 and consider what you want before figuring how much. Or just read the "guidelines" listed in Chapter 1 for measuring the particular product you want—tile (Pg. 1), carpet (Pg. 3), linoleum (Pg. 12). Then, if you are so inclined, delve into the examples given and see how the guidelines work and try them on your room.

The second half describes, in layman terms, how the floor you choose should be installed. If you are going to do it yourself, I recommend you study the chapters pertaining to your product all the way through before starting. Even if you are doing a tackless installation, read about the loose-lay installation first. If you are planning to install an inlaid linoleum study the first part regarding rotogravure products. This way you will get a "feel" for the subject before you pick up your knife.

Finally, you will find Chapter 12 gives some information about keeping your new floor looking good. This chapter, along with the rest of the book, is written from personal experience. I have found the simple procedures given really work. It is not necessary to have long lists of chemicals available for every conceivable cleaning problem if the homeowner will be prepared and tackle various "emergencies" intelligently and as outlined.

So take a little time and look over the following chapters before making your floor covering decisions. It really will make choosing and installing your floor much less subject to guess work and, who knows, it could even help make your decorating search a lot of fun!

## ACKNOWLEDGEMENTS

While this book was written from personal experience I nevertheless wish to express my special thanks to those who have contributed so much help and advice along the way.

For reviewing the contents of this book I especially want to thank Norton Hirsch of Balfred Floor Covering for his suggestions regarding product information, Bill Huegel for his thoughts about carpet installation and Charlie Picardy and Harold Bruni who gave me a number of tips for linoleum and tile installation. Thanks also to Richard Hopper of the Carpet and Rug Institute, Dalton, Georgia, for steering me to a number of sources of information.

And, for the use of their material in this book and their eagerness to help:

E.A. Denaut, Marketing, Alexander Smith Carpet, Amsterdam, N.Y.

Betsy J. Annese, Public Relations Manager, Bigelow Carpets, Bigelow-Sanford, Inc., Greenville, S.C.

David T. Lipton, Carpet Cushion Council, Farmington Hills, Mich.

Bill Walker, Sales Manager, and Millard Crain, Jr., General Manager, Crain Cutter Co., Inc. Santa Clara, Calif.

Faith A. Wohl, Public Affairs Manager, E.I. du Pont de Nemours & Co., Inc., Wilmington, Del. 19898

Esther Eisman, Manager of Marketing and Product Service,, Earl Grissmer Company, Inc. (Manufacturers of the RINSENVAC system.)

John B. Gundlach, General Manager, Beno J. Gundlach Co., Box 544, Belleville, Ill. 62222

Lee Kolker, Vice President/Styling, Masland Carpets, C.H. Masland & Sons, Carlisle, Pa.

Alan L. Malis, Milliken Carpets, LaGrange, Ga.

Larry Skiles, Roberts Consolidated Industries, City of Industry, Calif.

Raymond S. Jelly, Allied Chemical, Fibers Division, N.Y., N.Y.

Robert C. deCamara, Director of Press Services, Armstrong Cork Co., Lancaster, PA.

# 1 Measuring

When you go shopping at a lumberyard you usually know what you need and how much. But, are you similarly armed with knowledge, gained by experience or otherwise, when you go shopping at a floor covering store? Do you know what product you want to buy? And, most important, do you know how *much* you need?

If you are like most people, you don't. You leave it up to the floor covering dealer to tell you how much carpet, linoleum, or tile you require. You might get more than one estimate from various dealers and go with the one who seems most honest, or has given the lowest figure. Unfortunately, however, this is not always best. In most industries there are various ways of pulling the wool over the customer's eyes, and if the customer has no idea how to figure what is required, the possibility is all the more likely.

If you are able to walk into a floor covering store and say with authority, "I need 23 square yards of carpet," and show the dealer an accurate diagram of the area you want to cover and how you think it should be installed, you will command more respect than the average individual entering that store. I hasten to say that there may be more than one way to install your floor covering, especially if a complicated floor plan is involved. The dealer may have another, equally valid suggestion as to how it should be done. Once you understand the principles involved in measuring for floor covering, you will be able to talk intelligently with the dealer about alternatives.

This chapter will outline certain guidelines you need to understand to measure your floor for the particular product you are interested in. Some simple diagrams are included to illustrate how these guidelines apply to actual floor plans.

To measure your room you will need pencil, paper, and a tape measure or ruler of some sort. Any measuring device will do, but a steel tape measure 12 feet long or longer is best. Since I am measuring all sorts of areas all day long I use a 25-foot tape. This saves the trouble of marking short lengths on the floor and adding them up, and reduces the chance of making a mistake. If possible use graph paper, especially if you are measuring a complicated area.

## MEASURING FOR TILE

1. Measure to the widest and longest points in your room—such as into doorways.

2. Add at least 3 inches to each measurement to allow a margin for error and leeway for trimming.

3. Most asphalt, vinyl asbestos, solid vinyl, linoleum, and carpet tiles are sold by the square foot. A square foot covers 144 square inches. In

floor covering measurements, a square foot is not necessarily an area which is square and bounded by four 12-inch-long sides. It can be a narrow strip 2 inches by 72 inches, or 4 inches by 36 inches, and so forth. For measuring purposes, a square foot is 144 square inches regardless of its shape. To figure your actual square footage, multiply the length of the room by its width as determined in guidelines 1 and 2.

4. Eliminate from your calculations any significant sections which, though they may be a part of the room, are not actually part of the floor.

5. In complicated areas, say a kitchen plus pantry and hall, break down the various floor spaces into their individual squares or rectangles and add these together for the total footage required.

6. Tiles come in various sizes. Most are 12-by-12-inch squares. Quite a few also come in 9-by-9-inch squares. Some are 18 by 18, 3 by 9, and so forth. In many instances it is the pattern in the tile that dictates the size of the tile. Whatever size they may come in, they usually are sold by the square foot. If you tell your dealer that you need 177 square feet of tile, that is how many feet you will get—or as close to that amount as possible.

7. Many tiles are available only by the carton. Most cartons (of whatever size tile) contain 45 square feet. That is the first point where an accumulation of 9-by-9-inch tiles equals an even number of square feet and can be crated without cutting any tiles. Many dealers do not stock tile and can only order it by the carton. They will, therefore, have to sell the full cartons to you. With solid vinyl tile, however, the dealer may be able to help you; with the more expensive tiles, the dealer's supplier will usually "break" a carton and ship exactly what is ordered. There is normally a nominal fee for breaking a carton.

8. Always order a few extra tiles in case you make a few mistakes while installing, or in case your floor needs repairing over the years. With these principles in mind, let's see how much tile is called for in Figures 1-1 through 1-5.

**Guidelines for Figure 1-1:**

1. The room measures exactly 9 feet 9 inches by 12 feet 9 inches.

2. After adding 3 inches to each of the measurements, the room measures 10 feet by 13 feet.

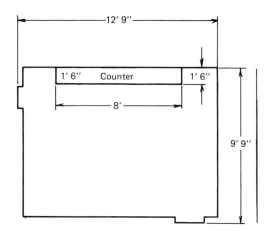

**Fig. 1-1**

3. You will be ordering by the square foot. Here, 10 by 13 equals 130 square feet.

4. Subtract the counter space. One foot 6 inches times 8 feet equals 12 square feet, and 130 − 12 = 118 square feet.

5. Not applicable.

6. The actual number of tiles you receive will vary according to the size of the tile you have chosen, but the square footage to be covered remains the same, and that amount is what you should order.

7. If your tile is available only by the carton, you will have to order three cartons, or 135 square feet (3 × 45 = 135).

8. You had better order a few extra tiles—bringing your order to 125 square feet. If you have to order by the carton, then the 3 cartons, or 135 square feet determined in number 7, should be fine.

**Guidelines for Figure 1-2:**

1. Basic areas are 3 feet 3 inches by 11 feet 9 inches, 5 feet 9 inches by 5 feet 9 inches, and 8 feet 9 inches by 10 feet 9 inches.

2. After adding 3 inches to each of these dimensions, the measurements become 3 feet 6 inches by 12 feet, 6 feet by 6 feet, and 9 feet by 11 feet.

3. You will be ordering by the square foot. Here your areas equal 42, 36, and 99 square feet respectively.

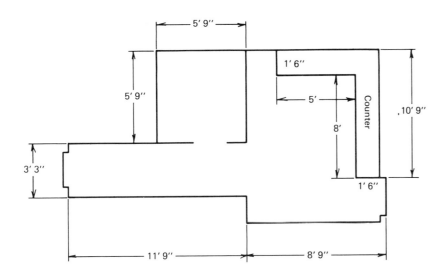

**Fig. 1-2**

4. However, you should subtract the counter space ($5' \times 1'6'' + 8' \times 1'6'' = 19.5$ square feet). This subtracted from the basic room area of 99 square feet gives a total of 79.5 square feet.

5. $42 + 36 + 79.5 = 157.5$ square feet.

6. You will order 158 square feet of tile, regardless of the size tile you have chosen.

7. If your tile is available only by the carton, you will order four boxes or 180 square feet.

8. If you are not ordering by the carton, you had better order 165 or 170 square feet.

## MEASURING FOR CARPET

1. Measure to the widest and longest points in your room—such as into doorways.

2. Add 3 inches or more to each measurement as a margin for error, for final trimming, and for an industry standard that allows as much as a 3-inch tolerance on carpet widths.

3. When measuring more than one area, say two or more rooms, draw a careful diagram showing how each area connects. This can be very important for determining in which direction you should spread your carpet. The reason for this will become apparent as you proceed.

4. Most carpet roll goods (as opposed to tiles) are sold by the square yard. A square yard equals 9 square feet. Normally, a square yard is thought of as a square bounded by 3-foot sides ($3 \times 3 = 9$ square feet). However, when it comes to floor covering, an area which may be 9 *inches* wide and 12 *feet* long is also the equivalent of a square yard.

5. The width in which the carpet you desire is available (not the dimension of your floor) determines how many square yards of carpet you will need. Carpet is manufactured in rolls. Most carpets are made only 12 feet wide, although some are made on looms which vary in width from 27 inches (2 feet 3 inches) wide on up. Back in the good old days, all looms were the 27-inch variety, and the rolls of carpet were sewn together to create wider widths; 4 feet 6 inches, 6 feet 9 inches, 9 feet, and so forth. Today most carpets are manufactured on broader looms—up to 15 feet wide—hence the term *broadloom*. Most carpets are made 12 feet wide. However, there are some 12 and 15 feet wide, some 15 feet only, and there still are some made 9 feet, 6 feet, 4 feet 6 inches, etc. Some highly specialized looms make varying odd widths of carpet. It is sometimes possible to have certain carpets woven to the exact dimensions of your room. Needless to say, this is very expensive.

For your purposes, however, you should figure that any carpet you might consider will be available 12 feet wide. Keep in mind that other widths may be available, especially 15 feet. But the common denominator in carpet is 12 feet.

6. You will need to figure how the available width (i.e., 12 feet) fits best into your layout both aesthetically and with as little waste as possible.

7. Multiply the dimensions of the carpet you have chosen to determine the number of square yards of material required. With these guidelines

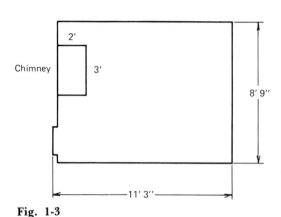

**Fig. 1-3**

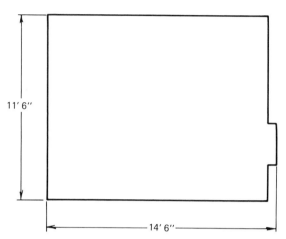

**Fig. 1-4**

in mind, let's see how much carpet the following diagrams call for:

**Guidelines for Figure 1-3:**

1. Taking contours and doorways into account, your room measures a net of 8 feet 9 inches by 11 feet 3 inches.

2. After adding 3 inches for error and trim, the dimensions are 9 feet by 11 feet 6 inches.

3. Not applicable.

4. You must determine the number of square yards of carpet required to cover your floor in the most efficient and least wasteful manner.

5. Your carpet is available 12 feet wide.

6. Which way does the 12-foot width of the carpet fit best into your room? Which will leave you with the least amount of waste? Eleven feet 6 inches subtracted from 12 leaves considerably less waste than 9 feet subtracted from 12. Therefore, tell the dealer you want a piece of carpet 12 feet by 9 feet from the 12-foot-wide roll. This may sound as if you have gotten your terms turned around—width has become length and length has become width. But the dealer and manufacturer are used to thinking in terms of the "width" of the rolls from which your carpet will be cut, not the width of your room. So they have to know whether you want a 12 by 9, 12 by 10, 12 by 11, and so forth. Tell the dealer you want a 12 by 9.

7. How many square yards are in a 12 by 9? (12 × 9 = 108 square feet, and 108 ÷ 9 = 12 square

yards.) You cannot subtract the square footage of the chimney in this room. This becomes a "cutout," and waste; perhaps you can use it as a doormat. Your actual room measurements were 9 feet by 11 feet 6 inches. If you multiply 9 times 11.5 and divide by 9, you get 11.5 square yards. So there will be waste no matter how you look at it. Since rolls only come in certain widths, and you have to allow something for trimming and possible mistakes, it is almost impossible to avoid at least some waste.

**Guidelines for Figure 1-4:**

1. Your room measures a net of 11 feet 6 inches by 14 feet 6 inches.

2. Adding 3 inches to each measurement gives you 11 feet 9 inches by 14 feet 9 inches to work with.

3. Not applicable.

4. You must determine the number of square yards of carpet required.

5. Your carpet is available 12 and 15 feet wide.

6. You can order a piece of carpet 12 feet by 14 feet 9 inches—an almost perfect fit with practically no waste. However, you might discover that the carpet you want is not available in the 12-foot width (perhaps it is out of stock). Therefore, you should see if it is available in a 15-foot width and in stock. If so, you can order a piece 15 feet by 11 feet 9 inches.

7. If you order 12-foot-wide goods, you will need to figure 12 + 14.75 (9 inches = ¾ of a foot) ÷ 9 =

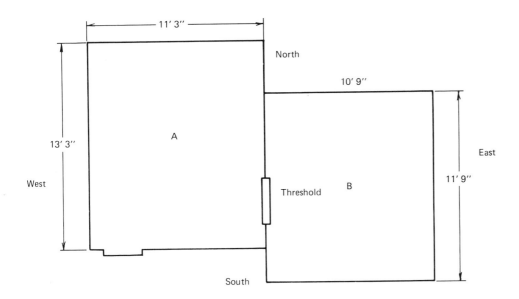

Fig. 1-5

19.67 square yards or 19²/₃ square yards. If you order the 15-foot width, then 15 × 11.75 ÷ 9 = 19.58 square yards—a slight saving.

This example demonstrates the need to keep different possible roll widths in mind, even though it is true today that most carpets come only 12 feet wide. You can find out what widths are available by checking the label of the carpet sample you are considering or by asking your dealer.

**Guidelines for Figure 1-5:**

1. You have two connecting rooms with a wooden threshold in the connecting doorway. The rooms measure:
Room A: 11′3″ × 13′3″
Room B: 10′9″ × 11′9″

2. Adding 3 inches these measurements become:
Room A: 11′6″ × 13′6″
Room B: 11′ × 12″

3. You have drawn a diagram (Fig. 1-5) using the measurements in number 2. How you lay out the carpet will depend on whether you use the same quality and color in both rooms and whether the carpet has a pattern in it requiring your attention.

4. You must determine the number of square yards required to cover both rooms.

5. Your carpet is available 12 feet wide.

6. The best fit with 12-foot-wide material is:
12′ × 13′6″ for Room A
12′ × 11′ for Room B
If you are using two different colors, this will be the best way to order the carpet.

7. 12 × 13.5 ÷ 9 = 18 square yards for Room A
12 × 11 ÷ 9 = 14.67 square yards for Room B

12 × 24.5 ÷ 9 = 32.67 square yards for both rooms.

However, if you are using the same quality and color of carpet then you must note that the solution in number 7 puts the carpet into room A with the pattern or nap (see number 12 under Seams) of the carpet running from north to south, while room B's carpet runs from east to west. This could prove visually disturbing in the doorway. You will have to decide whether the threshold between the two rooms separates the carpet enough so that the difference in direction does not matter.

If you are concerned about the difference in direction, you will need to order:

Room A: 12 × 12′6″ = 18 Yards
Room B: 12 × 12     = 16 Yards

Total:    12 × 25′6″ = 34 Yards

You may feel that keeping the pattern running in the same direction is worth the extra yardage.

**Fig. 1-6** Nap is falling in direction of arrow.

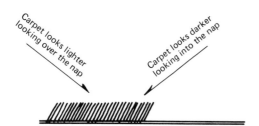

**Fig. 1-7**

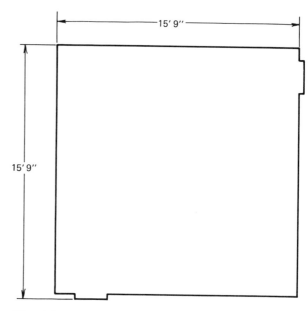

**Fig. 1-8**

### SEAMS

In addition to the basic seven principles outlined in Measuring Carpets, you should keep in mind the following five additions. Some of these rules do not apply in every installation, and one can cancel out another. Therefore, some judgment on your part may be required. The ideal installation plan would observe the seven basic rules. The following rules are numbered starting with number eight to remind you that all the previous guidelines are to be kept in mind as well.

8. If you can avoid it, do not put seams under a window. A seam is less likely to be visible in a section of the floor where there is less light.

9. Keep seams out of high-traffic areas. Seams in low traffic areas are less vulnerable to problems later on.

10. If possible, put the seam under a couch or other piece of furniture.

11. Check the direction of the nap and keep it all running the same way when piecing the carpet together.

The nap is the face yarn of the carpet upon which you walk. It usually has a tendency to lie or fall over in one direction. Check its direction by running your hand over the top of the carpet. That direction which gives your hand the least resistance

is the direction in which the nap is falling (running). If you do not keep the nap running in the same direction as you install each piece, the carpet can look as though it is two different colors. The light in your room reflects off the face of the carpet, which always looks lighter when you look over the nap and darker when you look into the yarn. If you put carpet together with the nap running in different directions you get different color impressions at the seam. Some carpets are more "forgiving" than others in this respect, but you should avoid nap reversal unless the pieces are going to be hidden.

12. Put your floor covering together with as few seams as possible. The following diagrams illustrate how these considerations apply to specific installations. At this point we will assume that you have the basics in mind and will not attempt a rule-by-rule discussion.

After three inches is added for safety, the room in Fig. 1-8 will need a carpet which, when it has been put together, will be 16 feet by 16 feet. Since 15 feet is almost 16 feet it might seem that you should order some floor covering that is 15 by 16 and then add on a foot that will, when you swing it around, fill out the side. To do this, you will order an extra piece 15 feet by 1 foot. But you need a piece that is 16 feet by 1 foot, so you will

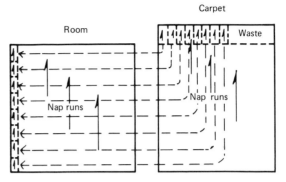

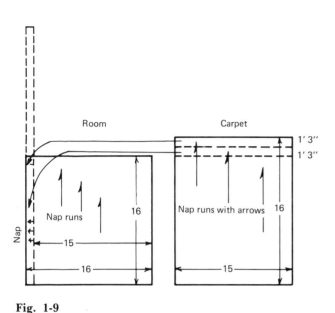

Fig. 1-9

Fig. 1-10

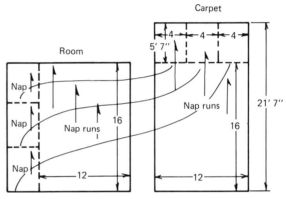

Fig. 1-11

need to order yet another strip 15 feet by 1 foot. When you add on 3 inches for trimming to each of your additional 1-foot cuts, you will be ordering an additional 2 feet 6 inches by 15 feet to fill out your 1-by-16-foot section—a total of 15 feet by 18 feet 6 inches for the entire room.

If you do install your floor covering in the manner just described, look at what you will have done! You will have changed the direction in which the nap is running by 90 degrees. It is true that this would be the easiest way to install the carpet with the fewest number of seams, but the change in nap direction might be noticeable and unattractive. You might get away with it if you are dealing with a shag carpet and if the seam is going to be under a couch. Be sure you know what you are doing before following this route.

What you should do is go by guideline number 12 and plan from the start to keep the nap or pattern running in the same direction. One way to do this with your 15-by-18-foot-6-inch piece would be to cut off the 2 feet 6 inches of extra flooring and then cut that piece into sections each one of which is 1 foot 3 inches wide by 2 feet 6 inches long. Then lay these out end to end until they add up to the 16 feet of length you need. This keeps everything running in the same direction, but you will be piecing together an unholy number of seams.

How about trying 12-foot goods? First, you'll need to order a piece 12 feet by 6 feet. This will leave a gap 4 feet by 16 feet to be filled (16 − 12 = 4). Four goes into 12 three times. This means that you can divide a 12-foot-wide piece of carpet into three pieces 4 feet wide, lay them end to end, and create a 16-foot-long piece. Sixteen feet divided by 3 equals 5 feet 4 inches. Adding 3 inches for trim gives you 5 feet 7 inches, so you'll need to order 12 feet by 16 feet plus 5 feet 7 inches, or a total of 12 feet by 21 feet 7 inches. Twelve feet times 21 feet 7 inches equals about 258 square feet. This, divided by 9, equals 28.67 square yards—that's practically a net fit with no waste.

## MORE THAN ONE ROOM

Following is a diagram of a house to be measured for carpet.

The material to be used only comes 12 feet wide. Note that the living room is 14 feet by 22

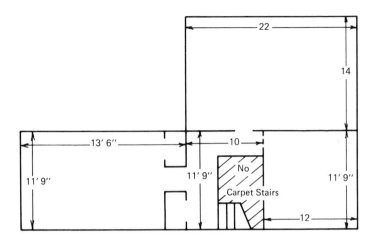

**Fig. 1-12**

feet. There are also stairs to be covered. (We'll get to stairs shortly in this chapter.) Note that the other three areas, two rooms and an entrance hall, are all almost 12 feet wide in the same direction. It might at first appear that you should run one piece of floor covering the length of the house (which adds up to almost 36 feet) through the two rooms and the entrance, and cut the length at the doorways to facilitate handling, then seam the pieces back together during installation. You might then cut another 22-foot length for the living room, ordering extra carpet to fill out the 2 feet needed to make up the 14-foot width. The waste from the stairway cutout, plus more to be ordered might go on the stairs.

But this scheme would mean a 22-foot-long seam, and in order to keep the nap running in the same direction it would require putting together several pieces end to end. Another look at your diagram can show you a better way. The length of the house is almost 36 feet. Twelve goes into 36 exactly 3 times. By turning the direction of the goods 90 degrees you can put it into the two rooms and hall in three pieces, each 12 feet wide by the 12-foot length common to each of the three areas. You can then turn the carpet in the living room and run it in with only two pieces, each 12 feet by 14 feet. You will now have only a 14-foot-long seam going across the room. This means you are putting two pieces of carpet 12 feet wide by 14 feet long side by side, creating a piece 24 feet by 14 feet. This leaves a 2-by-14-foot piece of waste to be cut off one edge. This piece can go on the stairs. So you end up using about the same amount of carpet for the installation with much less piecing-out.

What about the location of that seam in the living room? Say you are dealing with a short shag which you know will make an excellent seam—not visible unless you know exactly where it is. And, finally, say you have a number of large pieces of furniture (big, contemporary, overstuffed chairs) scattered about the room (not just along the walls) that cover much of the seam. Therefore, you may decide the seam across the room will not be a problem.

You have to analyze each situation with regard to your particular requirements. It is useful to make a diagram on graph paper and study it, keeping your needs and the type and quality of goods to be installed in mind before deciding how to put it in.

**PATTERN MATCHING**

Most carpets have no pattern that you need to consider when measuring. However, some do (such as many kitchen or so-called "indoor/outdoor" carpets). If the carpet you are considering does require pattern matching, you have to learn the principles involved. These principles or guidelines are discussed in the section on measuring for linoleum (since most linoleums do have patterns). You will want to keep all those guidelines in mind when measuring for your carpet. However, while most linoleums come 6 feet wide, most carpets are only available 12 feet wide. Therefore, you will need to adapt some of the discussion to the width of the material you are considering.

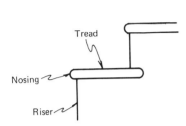

**Fig. 1-13**

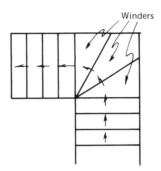

**Fig. 1-14** Nap or pattern direction (indicated by arrows) changes as steps change.

## STAIRS

Basically, there are three ways to cover a staircase. One is to install a runner up the center of the stairs, leaving a portion of the wooden step exposed on each side of the runner. The second is to install your floor covering wall to wall, if there are walls along both edges of the steps, and wall to banister where there is a banister instead of a wall on one or both sides of the steps. In the second method, you cover the entire step except for that portion which lies in between and outside the rungs of the banister. The third is to "upholster" the steps. In this case you literally cover every square inch of the stair tread and riser, including between the banister rungs and on the outside of the banister, and wrap the ends of the treads.

A step is composed of a tread, a nosing, and a riser. The tread is the portion you walk on. The riser is the board mounted vertically between each of the treads, and the nosing is the part of the tread that overhangs (or sticks out from) the riser. Some staircases have no nosing. This is of little concern as far as measuring is concerned.

Staircases can be broken down into four types. First, there is the straight staircase which is completely enclosed by walls on both sides—no banister or exposed ends of steps. Second is the staircase which is enclosed on one side but open on the other side, with a banister running down that edge. Third is the staircase which is a combination of the first two. Perhaps the first five steps are open on one or both sides with a banister, but the rest are between walls as they proceed to the next story. Fourth is the further complication which can be found in all three of the other types. That is the winding staircase. After going up three or four steps, winding staircases turn to the right or left,

usually at a right angle, giving you two or three odd-shaped steps that are called *winders*.

Whenever you measure for steps it is a good idea to follow the basic principle of keeping the nap or grain of the goods (number 12 under Seams) running in the same direction.

It is very disturbing to climb a flight of steps and find that, say halfway up, the installer has changed the direction of the material. This can be especially displeasing in a level-loop tweed carpet. With some carpets the nap direction on stairs may not matter, but with others it really does. Always keep the pattern, grain, or nap direction in mind while measuring.

Where winders are involved, nap direction takes on an added twist because the steps change direction. Here, you should follow the principle of running the nap on the nosing in the same direction as it runs on the steps directly below and above. For instance, if the carpet is installed on the bottom step with the grain up and down, then it will run up and down on each succeeding step. When you reach the first winder it will still run up and down on the nosing of that step. If the winder has turned 45 degrees, then the carpet direction will turn 45 degrees. On the next winder, which completes the 90-degree turn of the staircase, the goods will still run up and down on that step. Now the carpet direction has changed 90 degrees along with the staircase.

With all this in mind, let's do some measuring. Assume you have a straight staircase (no winders) which is 3 feet wide from wall to wall or banister. You are going to install a runner, leaving a border of exposed steps on either side of the carpet.

Further, assume you have twelve stair treads plus a top landing or hall which has a thirteenth riser beneath it. You want to cover all of the treads

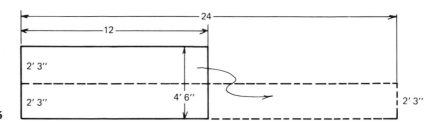

**Fig. 1-15**

and risers, starting with the first riser below the bottom tread and finishing with the thirteenth riser above the twelfth tread.

First, determine how wide you want your runner to be. For the moment, assume it will be 2 feet 3 inches wide. This will leave 4½ inches of stair tread exposed on each side of the runner. A 2-foot-3-inch runner is still a relatively common width. You may have found such a runner at a store. In this case, measure the distance to be covered from the very bottom of the first riser to the very top of the top riser by running a tape measure along the entire distance, making it conform to the contours of the riser, nosing, and tread just as the carpet will. Add a few inches to your final measurement for safety. You may want to fold the ends of your runner under at the top and bottom, so you'll need an extra inch or two for each fold.

You'll probably find, as you measure your treads and risers, that each complete step (riser plus tread) equals about 1½ feet. Therefore, a set of twelve steps will total about 18 feet plus the measurement of the top riser (1½ × 12 = 18). You should check the actual measurements of each step, as they can vary. If yours is an average set of steps, you will probably require about 19 feet of runner—18 feet plus around 8 or 9 inches for the top riser, plus a few inches for folding the ends comes to about 19 feet.

Now suppose you want to install your runner with exposed border, as just described, but you have not found a 27-inch-wide runner already made up by a manufacturer. The quality, style and color of carpet you want is only available in broadloom which comes 12 feet wide. What should you do? Just remember that you can take carpet which comes 12 feet wide and make it into almost any size you want, including a 27-inch-wide stair runner.

You want a runner which is 2 feet 3 inches (27 inches) wide and 19 feet long. How do you get this

out of a roll of carpet that is 12 feet wide? One way is to cut off a piece of carpet 12 feet by 2 feet 3 inches twice. This will make a total cut from the 12-foot-wide roll of 4 feet 6 inches. And that is what you should order—a piece 12 feet by 4 feet 6 inches. You then split it into two runners each 2 feet 3 inches by 12 feet. Putting these two pieces end to end gives you a runner 2 feet 3 inches by 24 feet—5 more feet than you really need. The extra piece might come in handy as an extra hall runner or entrance mat.

However, there is another, less wasteful way to install this runner. A roll of carpet can be split into runners each of which is as long as the entire roll of carpet. For instance, a 12-by-100-foot-long roll can be split into two rolls, each 6 by 100 feet long, or four rolls, each 3 feet wide.

You, of course, want a runner which is only 2 feet 3 inches wide by 19 feet long. But you can make use of the above example in your figuring.

Two feet 3 inches divides into 12 feet 5⅓ times. This means you can get five and one-third runners 2 feet 3 inches wide by 100 feet long out of a split roll. The one-third comes off the edge of the 12-foot-wide roll as waste, so you get only five complete runners. Since you can get five runners out of 12 feet, you can divide 5 into your desired 19 feet of length. Your answer is 3.8 feet, or almost 4 feet. This means that in theory you can order a 12-by-4-foot piece of carpet, split it into five pieces, put them end to end, and have a 20-foot runner—one foot longer than you really need. However, you should always join stair runners only at the point where the tread meets the riser of the next step (at the back of the tread). In short, any piece of carpet to be installed on steps should cover at least one complete step.

Average stairs require 1 foot 6 inches of carpet for each complete step. Therefore, two steps require 3 feet of runner, three steps will require 4 feet 6 inches, and so forth. If you were to order

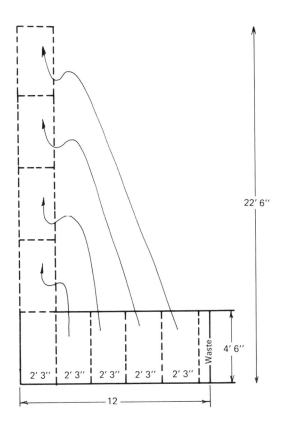

22' 6"

4' 6"

Waste

2' 3"  2' 3"  2' 3"  2' 3"  2' 3"

12

**Fig. 1-16**

only 4 feet by 12 feet, you would find that after splitting the 12 feet into five runners, each 2 feet 3 inches by 4 feet, your runners would only complete two steps each. You would, therefore, only be able to cover ten out of your twelve steps, and you would be left with four pieces of waste. So you had better order a piece of carpet 4 feet 6 inches by 12 feet, and you really should add on a couple of extra inches for good measure. Therefore, your actual order should be for a piece 12 feet by 4 feet 6 or 9 inches.

As far as this last example is concerned there is one more possible problem. As you will see in Chapter 7, some carpets require that cut edges be bound or protected in some manner and some do not. If the one you have chosen does not require binding or protection, the previous discussion contains what you need to know about measuring for your flight of stairs. If, however, your edges are likely to have a problem, you will either need to have them bound before installation, or you can take the very easy way out of folding the edges

under. This means, though, that you will need pieces more than 2 feet 3 inches wide in order to have a finished runner of that width. You will need about 1½ inches extra on each edge to be able to fold it under successfully—a total of 3 inches more. Therefore, in the first example, instead of ordering 2 feet 3 inches of width two times for a total of 4 feet 6 inches, you will need 2 feet 6 inches twice for a total of 5 feet. If you follow the second example of turning the carpet 90 degrees, you will find that you can get five runners out of 12 feet, each one about 2 feet 5 inches wide. With this you can have the width you want without ordering any extra material. If you should find that the carpet comes through, say, only 11 feet 10 inches wide, you might have to compromise a bit on the width of your runner. But the basic effect of a 2-foot-3-inch runner still could be achieved.

You should keep these options in mind as you start measuring various staircases. The way you lay carpet out on stairs can often make quite a difference in the amount you need to buy.

Measuring a straight staircase to figure wall-to-wall or wall-to-banister coverage is not much different from the runner approach. You are simply making a wider runner that will cover all of the step. All you need to do in the case of a wall-to-wall staircase (with no banister) is measure the width of the entire stair tread and add an inch or two for good measure to determine the width of the carpet runner you will need. If your staircase is 3 feet wide, you can order enough carpet by getting a piece 12 feet by 6 feet plus a couple of inches for safety. You can split this into a runner 3 feet by 24 feet.

In this case, though, 3 feet divides exactly into 12. So you might try turning your carpet 90 degrees and splitting the 12-foot-wide carpet into four runners which can go end to end on your stairs. A piece 12 feet by 4 feet 6 inches gives you exactly three steps per runner or twelve steps, but not that top riser. If, however, you order 5 feet 3 inches, you will have some margin for error on the length of each of your runners plus enough for the top riser, and you will have to buy 1 square yard of carpet less than with the first approach. You should check the width of the stairs to be sure that you will not be in trouble if the carpet comes through a little less than 12 feet wide.

Suppose you have a complicated staircase that you want to cover wall to wall. You will need to divide the staircase into components, each of which will require a different size "runner." Assume that a flight of twelve steps has three at the bottom which are 4 feet wide, then three individual winders, and then five steps, each 3 feet wide. In effect, you will need one runner 4 feet wide by the length required for three steps ($3 \times 1'6'' = 4'6''$) or a piece 4 feet by 4 feet 6 inches plus a few inches for good measure. Each of the winders will probably have to be figured separately, with each one requiring what is in effect a separate runner. The top five steps will need a runner 3 feet wide by 7 feet 6 inches plus a foot as a margin for error and to cover the top riser.

Now let's say you are going to upholster this staircase. This means you are going to run the carpet across the treads as just described, but you are going to continue it through the rungs of the banister and over the ends of the treads, finishing it off under the treads. All this means from the measuring point of view is that you will need an even wider runner. Instead of 4 feet from wall to banister you may need 4 feet 6 inches. Other than that, all the previously explained methods of figuring apply.

Sometimes it helps to take a piece of graph paper and plot out a 12-foot-wide piece of carpet on it, then start putting the various dimensions into it until you find the configuration that fits best. One thing is certain, though. Stairs, especially winders, involve waste. You'll always be left with marvelous triangles of carpet that you won't be able to use.

You may be using the same carpet in other areas besides the staircase. Be sure you keep track of what waste will be coming out of the other rooms, and see how it could go on the stairs. You might find that each step will have to be done individually, but doing so will use up a lot of the waste. For instance, in Fig. 1-12 there is waste from the living room that is 2 feet by 14 feet. The steps are 2 feet 9 inches wide by 1 foot 6 inches each. The waste piece covers four steps, 2 feet 9 inches by 2 feet each. This does not use all the waste, but enough to be worthwhile.

## MEASURING FOR LINOLEUM

Much of the discussion regarding measuring for carpet applies to measuring for linoleum as well, and you will find that the following principles

closely parallel those outlined for carpet. Yet, there is enough difference between the two to consider them separately. You may want to refer back to the section on carpet for detailed explanations in order to fully appreciate the following discussion. Basic principles for measuring linoleum are:

1. Always measure to the widest and longest points in your room—such as into doorways.

2. Always add 3 inches or more to each measurement as a margin for error and for trimming.

3. When measuring more than one area, such as two or more rooms, draw a careful diagram showing how each area connects. This can be very important for determining in which direction your linoleum should be spread. The reason for this will become apparent as the discussion proceeds.

4. Most linoleum roll goods (as opposed to tile) are sold by the square yard. A square yard equals 9 square feet. Normally, this is thought of as a square bounded by 3-foot sides ($3 \times 3 = 9$ square feet). However, when it comes to linoleum, an area that is, for example, $1'6''$ wide and 6 feet long is the equivalent of a square yard.

5. The width in which the product you desire is available, not the dimensions of your floor, determines how many square yards of linoleum you need. Linoleum is manufactured in rolls. Most linoleums are made 6 feet wide, some 9 feet, many 12 feet, and a few 15 feet. You should assume that most linoleum will be available 6 feet wide, and quite possibly 12 feet wide. It is generally only in the cheaper lines that you will find 9-foot goods. As of this writing only Congoleum offers 15-foot goods, in their line called Spring.

6. You will need to figure how the available width (i.e., 6 feet) fits best into your layout both aesthetically and with as little waste as possible.

7. You must multiply the dimensions of the linoleum you choose (not the floor to be covered) to determine the number of square yards of material required.

With the above principles in mind, let's see how much linoleum the following diagrams call for.

## Guidelines for Figure 1-17:

Here is a small bathroom with tub. The tub rests on the floor, so you will not have to cover under it.

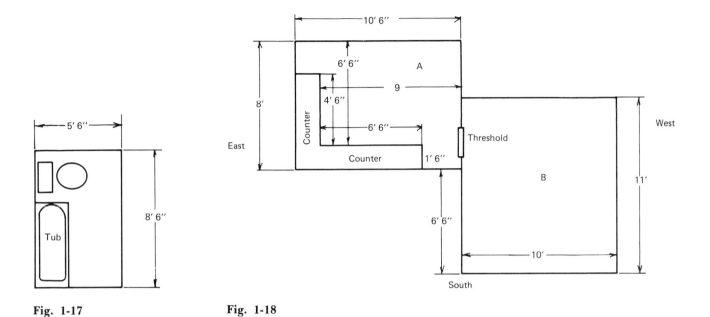

Fig. 1-17                      Fig. 1-18

1. The bathroom measures 5 feet 6 inches by 8 feet 6 inches.

2. After adding 3 inches, the basic area is 5 feet 9 inches by 8 feet 9 inches.

3. Not applicable.

4. How many square yards of linoleum do you require?

5. The material is available 6 feet wide.

6. Therefore, you will need to purchase a piece of linoleum that is 6 feet wide and 8 feet 9 inches long.

7. $6 \times 8'9'' = 52.5$ square feet $\div 9 = 5.83$ square yards. While the actual floor space (excluding the tub enclosure) equals a great deal less, you will have to order 5.83 square yards of linoleum.

## Guidelines for Figure 1-18:

Here is a kitchen with connecting dining area. A wooden threshold is in the doorway dividing the two rooms. You want the same patterned linoleum in both rooms.

1. You have two areas measuring 8 feet by 10 feet 6 inches and 10 feet by 11 feet respectively.

2. After adding for error, you need to cover basic floor spaces of 8 feet 3 inches by 10 feet 9 inches and 10 feet 3 inches by 11 feet 3 inches respectively.

3. You have diagrammed these dimensions and indicated where the kitchen counters will be. This could be very important, as you will see in later illustrations.

4. You need to know the number of square yards of linoleum required.

5. Your linoleum is available 6 feet and 12 feet wide.

6. If you are not concerned about whether the pattern in the linoleum will match in the doorway (remember the threshold that will separate the two rooms) then the best fit will be:

$12 \times 8'3''$ for room A
$\underline{12 \times 10'3''}$ for room B
$12 \times 18'6''$ total

This means that the pattern in the material will be turned at 90 degrees from room B to room A. If this matters to you, then you will need to consider obtaining:

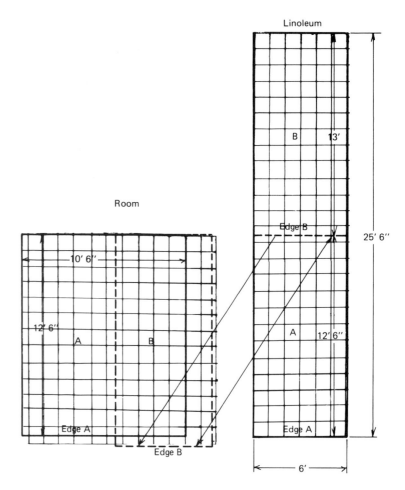

**Fig. 1-19**

12 ×  8′3″ for room A
<u>12 × 11′3″</u> for room B
12 × 19′6″ total

In both cases the counters become waste, and in the latter instance you may feel that it is worth buying an extra foot of material to keep the pattern running in the same direction. To keep the pattern lined up in the doorway between the two rooms, see the section on pattern matching.

  7.  12 × 18′6″ = 222 square feet ÷ 9 = 24.67 square yards.
      12 × 19′6″ = 234 square feet ÷ 9 = 26 square yards.

## SEAMS

Besides the basic principles for measuring linoleum, you should keep in mind the five addi-

tions that follow. As with the discussion of carpet, some of these rules do not apply in every installation, and one can cancel out another. Therefore, some judgment on your part may be required. An ideal installation plan would observe all these rules wherever possible. These principles are numbered starting with 8 to remind you that all the previous guidelines regarding linoleum have to be kept in mind too.

  8. Always add 3 inches to your measurements for each seam to allow a margin for error and for trimming.

  9. If you can avoid it, do not put seams under a window. A seam is less likely to be visible in a section of the floor where there is less light.

10. Keep seams out of high-traffic areas. In low-traffic areas, seams are less vulnerable to problems later on.

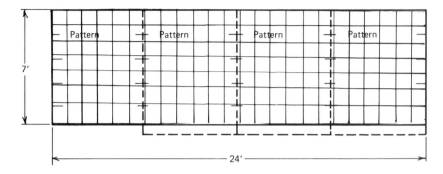

Fig. 1-20

11. If possible, put the seam under furniture.

12. Much of your figuring will depend on whether there is a repeat pattern in your linoleum. If there isn't, you can skip this part of the discussion. If there is, you must take the pattern into account when measuring. This is because when you install the linoleum, you will have to match the pattern along the edges where the pieces join to make a seam.

Most linoleums have a definite pattern which requires matching at the seams. Most linoleum samples tell you on the back whether there is a pattern and what its repeat is. Usually there is a 1-foot-6-inch repeat, but some patterns have as little as 1½ inches and some as much as 4 feet 6 inches. Sometimes a label will tell you that the pattern repeats every, say, 4 feet 6 inches, but has a 1-foot-6-inch match. This means you can match the goods every 1 foot 6 inches, and that is the figure you need to worry about. When you measure your room you must account for the repeat to be sure that, as you cut off each piece of linoleum and place it in the room, these points will line up properly.

Figure 1-19 shows a room that is 10 feet 6 inches wide and 12 feet 6 inches long, and a piece of linoleum that is 6 feet wide and 25 feet 6 inches long. Assume that the pattern repeat is 1 foot and that the grid lines in the graph paper represent the pattern. Your first cut off the linoleum is 12 feet 6 inches long, fitting perfectly into the length of the room. The dotted line in the linoleum indicates this cut. This piece is lettered A, and piece A has been placed in the room. Note, however, that the cut in the linoleum falls in the middle of the pattern. If you put the edge of piece B next to

piece A and line the edge of B up with the bottom edge of A along the same wall, the pattern repeat will be off by half of a repeat, or in this case, 6 inches. Therefore, you need to find the next point in piece B where the pattern will line up with the pattern in piece A. You have to shift B down 6 inches until the line on B lines up with the line on A along the bottom wall. Then you need another 12 feet 6 inches to make that piece extend all the way to the opposite wall. Piece B will have to be 13 feet long (6 inches plus 12 feet 6 inches) while piece A only needs to be the actual length of the room—12 feet 6 inches. The pattern repeat has made it necessary to buy 6 inches more material than would be required if there were no pattern.

In Fig. 1-20, you are measuring for a room 7 feet wide and 24 feet long. The pattern repeat is 1 foot 6 inches. This repeat falls along an edge of linoleum at 1 foot 6 inches, 3 feet, 4 feet 6 inches, 6 feet and 7 feet 6 inches. It does not fall at 7 feet. For each piece after the first, you must add to each measurement the amount needed to start each new piece at the same point in the pattern where the first piece started. In this case, the repeat falls at 7 feet 6 inches. For every piece you add to the first you will need an extra 6 inches of material in order to line it up with each previous piece. Whereas a linoleum with no pattern would call for four cuts, each 6 by 7 feet for a total of 6 by 28 feet, this requires one cut of 7 feet and three of 7 feet 6 inches, for a total of 6 feet by 29 feet 6 inches.

## Guidelines for Fig. 1-18 with Repeat and No Threshold

Now look back at Fig. 1-18 and assume that your linoleum is only available 6 feet wide, that there is no threshold between the two rooms, and that you have a linoleum with a 1-foot-6-inch pattern repeat.

See numbers 1 to 4 under Measuring for Linoleum except that here you will assume that 3 inches for error was added into the measurements before the diagram was labeled. Therefore, you need cuts to fill the dimensions as labeled.

5. Your linoleum is available only 6 feet wide.

6. This installation can be run either from south to north or from east to west in both rooms. Examine both, and you can decide which would be best. Keep all the principles in mind and draw on them as required. Start with the south to north approach.

Starting at the east wall of room A, you will need a 6-foot-6-inch piece to run from the north wall to the counter. For the next 6-foot-wide piece you will need a net of 8 feet, but you have to add enough to match a 1-foot-6-inch repeat. The match falls at 7 feet 6 inches and then at 9 feet but not at 8 feet. Therefore, your second piece will have to be 9 feet long. So for room A you will need 6 feet 6 inches plus 9 feet. When you actually install the linoleum, don't try to drop this last cut through the doorway, as that would be just about impossible. Instead, lay out the pieces with the right edge of the longer piece just dropping into the doorway, and the seam 6 feet to the left. There will be 1 foot 6 inches of waste off the east edge of the 6-foot-6-inch piece.

In room B, you will need 11 feet net to run the first piece next to the doorway from south to north. You also have to match the pattern at the doorway. The pattern will not fall at 11 feet but rather at 10 feet 6 inches or 12 feet, so you will have to go to 12 feet. Your last piece will require the same amount. There is one additional problem, however. There is no common wall between the two rooms—no common point from which each piece will start as you proceed from one cut to the next. In Fig. 1-20, for instance, you always started at exactly the same point along the 24-foot-long wall. Here, however, you cannot do that. The starting wall in room A bears no relation to the starting wall in room B. You will have to add one more pattern repeat to be sure that you can effect a match at the threshold. Here are the five measurements for this layout:

$6 \times 6'6''$
$6 \times 9'$
$6 \times 12'$
$6 \times 12'$
$\underline{6 \times 1'6''}$ (to match at doorway)
$6 \times 41 \div 9 = 27.33$ square yards.

Now try the east to west layout. Starting in room B, you will need a first cut of 10 feet to fill the south of the room. A seam will fall 6 feet from the south wall. Theoretically, a second piece could now be planned to run from the west wall of room B to the counter along the east wall of room A. This would call for a total of 19 feet. But a 1-foot-6-inch repeat falls at 19 feet 6 inches, not 19 feet. In addition, it will be very difficult to drop such a piece through the doorway with no seam at the doorway. Therefore, you had better add one pattern repeat so that you can break the goods and put it back together at that point. In theory you should be able to do this without any extra material, but most professionals would want this extra amount just in case, and you should figure on it too. So you should get 1 foot 6 inches in addition to the 19 feet 6 inches or a total of 21 feet. Finally, you will need a 10-foot-6-inch piece for filling out the north wall of room A, a perfect fit. However, remember that you have not started this piece at a wall which is common to the first two pieces. In fact, the starting wall of this last piece falls right in the middle of the pattern repeat. This means you must add on another repeat (1 foot 6 inches) for this last piece to go in correctly. Your total cut is now 6 by 12. This, of course, is incredibly wasteful; you are filling a 2-by-10-foot-6-inch area with a 6-by-12-foot piece of linoleum. How can you cut that down? You might split your 6-foot-wide material into two 3-foot-wide pieces and put them end to end. For instance, if the goods had no pattern, you could take 6 feet by 5 feet 3 inches and split that into two pieces 3 feet by 5 feet 3 inches. Put these end to end and you have 3 feet by 10 feet 6 inches. This creates a cross-seam, but it cuts the amount of material required by nearly half. (Not quite half, because you must add 3 inches to the measurement for the cross-seam).

The same principle works with a patterned linoleum. Here, you can figure on cutting the 12-foot length in half, getting 6 feet by 6 feet rather than 6 feet by 12 feet. Because you are adding a seam you will require an additional pattern repeat (1 foot 6 inches) to make sure of a match at the cross-seam. This last piece will have to be 6 feet by 7 feet 6 inches—still a lot better than 6 by 12, if you can tolerate this cross-seam. Here are the measurements for this layout:

$$6 \times 10'$$
$$21'$$
$$7'6''$$

$6 \times 38'6'' = 25.67$ square yards.

You will have to judge whether the lower yardage is worth two extra cross-seams and the consequently more difficult installation.

# 2 Carpet, Linoleum or Tile— Which to Buy and from Whom?

## FROM WHOM

Floor covering is one of the most highly competitive industries in the United States, if not in the world. More than 400 manufacturers and importers of linoleum, tile, carpet, and area rugs are listed in *Floor Covering Weekly*'s "Local Product Source Directory for 1978." All of these manufacturers vie for your dollar through some 1,100 wholesale distributors who, in turn, sell those products to you, the consumer, through thousands of large and small retail dealers throughout the country.

This structure breeds an incredibly competitive situation. While there are a number of associations for floor covering dealers, distributors, and manufacturers, enabling members to get together and to discuss mutual problems, there is no collusion or price fixing. On the contrary, it is often amazing to see the lengths these manufacturers, distributors, and retailers will go to in attempting to "beat each other out."

Most of this works to the consumer's advantage. First, there will always be low-priced floor covering available to the consumer. A mill may bring out an expensive new pattern, but if that pattern becomes popular, other mills often copy it at a lower price, bringing down the cost of the original.

The second advantage is, perhaps, more important. Because it is difficult for the mills to compete on price effectively over more than the short run, most of them compete very meaningfully on service. For example, while it may take six to eight weeks (or more) for you to receive an order of a new couch, a dealer can usually promise overnight delivery of floor covering from a local distributor or two to three week delivery if ordering directly from a mill. Of course, there are exceptions. Mills can have trouble keeping up with orders and, therefore, be out of stock, but delivery delays because of stock shortage don't happen very often.

Perhaps even more important than availability of stock is the willingness of the distributor and the manufacturer to stand behind their product. As with any machine-made item, floor covering can be defective. Even though it may take months for a problem to appear, you can count on the dealer to take care of any defect you have discovered because the dealer knows he/she can rely on the distributor and the manufacturer to stand behind the product 100 percent.

Normally a guarantee against manufacturing defects lasts one or two years, depending on the mill. If anything is intrinsically wrong with the product, it should show up within twelve months. After that period the dealer may have a more

**Full five year wear warranty.** All carpets bearing the ANSO label carry this wear warranty: This carpet is warranted for indoor use (residential or commercial depending on construction*) by the Fibers Division of Allied Chemical Corporation. If properly installed and maintained and the surface pile in any given area is abrasively worn more than 10% within 5 years, it will be replaced at our expense, including installation. Allied Chemical warrants abrasive wear *only,* not tears, pulls, cuts, pilling, shedding, matting, or damage due to improper cleaning agents or methods. By abrasive wear is meant fiber lost from the carpet. Stairs are excluded for cut-pile carpet.

**Full lifetime static warranty.** All carpets bearing the ANSO-X label also carry the following anti-shock warranty: This carpet is also warranted to control static electricity to a maximum of 3.5 kilovolts at a relative humidity of 20% and a room temperature of 70° F. (Test: AATCC 134-1975, option V, oak tanned leather soles). Should this carpet fail at any time during its useful life to achieve this performance, it will be replaced at our expense, including installation. If requested, one square yard of the carpet must be furnished for testing to verify any complaint of failure.
  For warranty service contact your ANSO® carpet dealer or Allied Chemical, Customer Service, Box 831, Hopewell, Virginia 23860. These warranties give you specific legal rights, and you may also have other rights which vary from state to state.

**Fig. 2-1** Anso warranty. (Courtesy Allied Chemical.)

difficult time getting a settlement. But if you really do have a legitimate complaint, the dealer will probably be able to work something out.

There are also an increasing number of carpets coming on to the market which have a five-year limited warranty. Normally these warranties are made by the manufacturer of the yarn which has been tufted into the carpet. Allied Chemical, for example, guarantees that carpet with Anso nylon will last in a residence for five years (with certain limitations) if the mill has followed specifications in constructing the carpet. Enkaloft makes a similar warranty, and so do several others. In most instances these warranties are quite carefully spelled out on a label on the back of the sample of carpet.

Whether a warranty will be honored can depend on the reliability of the dealer and the manufacturer. Because the industry is so highly competitive, there are always individuals trying to "get some of the action." Sometimes these individuals have been trained as installers by established dealers and then go into business themselves, freelancing their labor at first. Soon some find distributors who are willing to wholesale floor covering to them, and they go into business (perhaps out of a car) selling the product as well as installing it. They can sell at close to cost because they have no overhead (no store rent, payroll, taxes, advertising or other expenditures) and are primarily interested in selling their labor.

This is where the consumer really can get a buy. Unfortunately, this is also where the consumer can get taken. Normally, freelancers (known as "gypsies" in the trade) are perfectly sincere in their efforts to sell real value to their customers, but the mortality rate among this type of dealer is incredibly high. In their attempts to get your order they will sell too cheap. Suddenly they simply are unable to meet their daily expenses, or they decide it is simply not worth the effort. The average carpet installer has to be a hard worker in order to make a profit. Sometimes there isn't enough profit so he/she goes out of business.

Where does this leave you? Six months or a year after your floor was installed something goes wrong with it. Who do you turn to for service? The answer is, you don't, unless you are willing to pay an established dealer to come in and straighten out the situation.

## WHICH PRODUCT

There are certain basic thoughts which you should keep in the back of your mind when choosing a floor covering.

### What Color or Pattern?

A basic rule of interior decoration is to pick out your floor covering first, because your selection is much more limited than with paint and wallpaper. The selection process is much simpler if you start with the floor and work your way up.

The selection of color and pattern is a matter of personal taste, but if you would like assistance, it is available to you. Some stores have interior decorators whose services may even be free. Many decorator magazines are published monthly. You'll find a lot of them at various dealers and home product stores. These publications often have a wealth of helpful ideas.

Many stores also have personnel who, though not interior decorators, can still be quite helpful. Don't be afraid to ask. Often they will at least be able to keep you from making a big mistake in your choice of color or pattern.

In the last analysis, you will have to decide on color, pattern, type, and quality. Avoid impulse buying. Take samples home to be examined in the rooms where they will be used. This is most important, because the light in the store is invariably different from yours at home, and a color that looks great in the shop may be less pleasing in your house. Never rely on memory when matching colors; take the time to bring samples home so you can be sure of your decisions.

Some stores require a deposit for samples you take home. That is because the dealer has to pay for those samples if replacement becomes necessary. Your deposit is refunded when you return the samples.

In many instances, the salesperson will be glad to bring samples to you at home. Some dealers offer a shop-at-home service. They will bring their complete line of samples to your home and spend as much time as needed to help you decide what would be right for you. If a shop-at-home service is available, take advantage of it.

## WHAT TYPE OF FLOOR—CARPET, LINOLEUM, OR TILE?

So far this discussion has been limited to what would look nice. But what about the *type* of floor covering? What makes the most sense for your particular application? The following facts will assist you in reaching a practical decision in keeping with your personal taste.

First, because they are nonporous, linoleum and tile are generally easier to spot-clean than carpet. A carpet may be tightly woven and treated to resist soiling, but it still is more difficult to wipe away an egg from carpet than from linoleum. On the other hand, vacuuming a carpet daily or weekly is a lot easier than washing and scrubbing linoleum. Carpet is warmer and softer than linoleum. Many kitchen carpets are amazingly easy to clean. You have to decide which qualities are most important to you.

Second, it usually is easier to cover a floor's "sins" with carpet than with linoleum. An uneven floor still will be uneven after linoleum or tile have been laid over it, whereas a thick carpet and pad installed over the same floor will hide a great deal more. In fact, it normally is not wise to install linoleum over a seriously irregular floor unless you first put down a layer of underlayment board (see Chapter 6). Irregularities in the original floor will "telegraph" right through a thin piece of linoleum, tile, or thin carpet, for that matter.

Third, carpet, especially with pad, is usually more soundproofing than linoleum or tile. This is especially true where you may want to insulate the story below from the sound of footsteps on the floor to be covered. However, some of the heavily cushioned linoleums may prove satisfactory to you in this respect. Carpet also deadens sound within a room, as do drapes on walls. In addition, carpet, together with a dense, thick pad, can have considerable insulating and energy saving properties. A cold floor can be made considerably warmer with carpeting.

Fourth, tile is easier to install than roll goods. If you make a mistake in trimming you have only ruined one piece of tile, and that piece might be usable in another section of the floor where a small piece of tile is needed. As you will see in the do-it-yourself section, with roll goods carpet is usually easiest to install. This certainly is true of foam-backed carpet, especially foam-backed shag. Carpet is simply much more "forgiving" when you make a mistake than is linoleum. On the other hand, some of the new do-it-yourself linoleums are amazingly easy to install in many situations. They certainly are easier to install than most carpets that have to be placed over pads, permanently stretched in, and fastened down.

Fifth, allergies may be a problem in your family. If so, you may not want to install carpet, especially the shaggier types which can hold dust. Also, certain fibers in carpet may aggravate allergies, so you should consider this when making your choice. Some of the vinyls in linoleum can have slightly offensive odors. These normally dissipate quickly.

Finally, your budget probably governs what you can install in your room. You may wish that you could put down linoleum, but the condition of your floor may require repairs that are too costly to justify such an investment. A tightly woven kitchen type of carpet (often misnamed "indoor/outdoor") installed over a ½-inch-thick foam pad could be much less expensive. Of course, if the room is new or you have installed a new subfloor, you'll simply be concerned with looks and performance.

The next two chapters will consider the specific types of products that are available and what you can expect from them. In Chapter 3 we will discuss carpet. Chapter 4 will deal with linoleum and tile.

# 3 Types of Carpet and Padding

Even as this book is being written, a new style of carpet and another "revolutionary" concept in linoleum is probably being developed somewhere by someone. At times it seems almost impossible to keep up with the changes. However, there are certain basic facts regarding the construction of floor coverings which remain reasonably constant and of which you should be aware.

## HOW IS CARPET MADE?

Virtually all broadloom carpets are either woven or tufted. Most carpet for sale today is tufted, but there are still enough woven carpets on the market to warrant discussion.

Woven carpets are made on either Velvet, Axminster, Wilton, or knitting looms. The face yarns are woven into the back yarns in such a manner that the interweaving causes an interlocking that holds it all together. Weaving usually produces a very regular pattern of warp and woof yarns (which constitute the back) that is visible on the back of the carpet. The warp yarns run lengthwise and the woof yarns run across the width. These lines are often straight enough to follow when cutting the carpet.

Sometimes the manufacturer will apply a layer of latex adhesive to the back so that it will not tend to unravel on the cut edges. Even so, a woven carpet must be bound along any cut edge which is going to be left exposed, or it will unravel.

Tufted carpets look similar to woven carpets, but their construction is quite different. They are made by inserting the face yarn into a ready-made back. The yarn is held in the back with a coating of latex adhesive, then a second back is applied to give the product greater strength. This second back often looks like burlap and can give the carpet the appearance of being woven. Close inspection will reveal that the direction of the weave in the back bears no relation to the direction of the weave in the face. It may not even be straight, and this makes the carpet back appear to be way out of alignment with its edges. Careful measuring and use of a chalk line or straight edge is usually necessary when you cut this type of carpet.

Tufted carpet has some tremendous advantages over woven. For one thing, it can be manufactured much faster than woven carpet, making it less expensive. In fact, it was the advent of the tufting process, together with synthetic yarns, that began to make wall-to-wall carpet something most people could afford. In addition, tufting has made an incredible number of styles of carpet available that simply did not exist before. Another advantage is that many of today's tufted carpets can be cut in any direction, and do not require binding

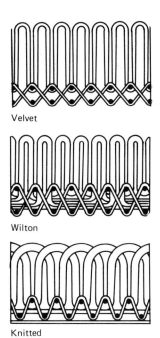

Velvet

Wilton

Knitted

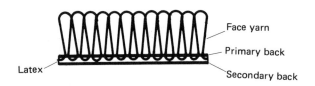

Face yarn

Primary back

Latex

Secondary back

**Fig. 3-2** Cross section of tufted carpet showing face yarn, primary back, secondary back, and latex adhesive between two backs.

**Fig. 3-1** Various types of woven carpets. Note interlocking of back yarns with face yarns.

because their edges will not unravel. Generally speaking, tufted carpets, being much more pliable, are much easier to install than woven carpets. The tufting process and developments arising out of it have made do-it-yourself carpet installation so popular today.

### Yarns

Carpet yarns are of two types—natural and synthetic. The most commonly used natural yarns are wool or cotton, but jute or hemp are used occasionally. In most instances, however, wool is the face yarn in broadloom carpet made of natural fibers. Wool is, in the opinion of many, still the finest yarn available. But advances made in the last decade in the manufacture of synthetic yarns have all but eliminated the so-called advantages of wool—especially when you compare cost.

Synthetics are nylons, polyesters, olefins, acrylics, and rayon. Not many carpets today contain rayon, but it may still be used in very inexpensive fabrics. This is because the the other synthetics pretty much outstripped rayon in performance.

The synthetic yarns (not including rayon) can be further classified as "first-generation" and "second-generation" yarns. The second-generation

yarns are later developments of the originals. For instance, Antron III is the most recent development in nylon created by Du Pont, Anso is the most recent nylon made by Allied Chemical, Herculon IV is the Hercules Corporation's most recent olefin fiber, and Trevira Star is the most recent of the polyesters produced by Hoechst Fibers Industries. All of these and many other second-generation yarns have the same thing in common: each is made in a new configuration which is supposed to give it a soil-hiding characteristic, greater durability, and more resilience.

Synthetics start as a liquid. It is then pulled through a sieve that is somewhat like the colander in your kitchen. The holes in the sieve are tiny. The liquid, as it comes through these holes, comes out in strands that are as thin as, or thinner than, a human hair. In first-generation yarns the strands were all round. Further, the strand was clear; a round strand tended to behave the same as a round glass of water. It would magnify what was on the other side, such as dirt in the carpet. In addition, the strand had little hairs sticking out of its sides that tended to hold onto minute dirt particles. The fact that some synthetics, especially nylon, had a tendency to develop static electricity added up to a real problem with dirt. The yarn acted as a magnet to attract dirt as well as to produce a shocking experience for the consumer.

Light source                    Reflected

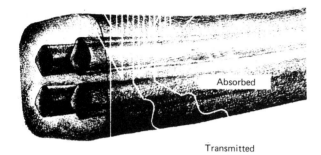

Absorbed

Transmitted

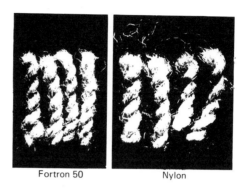

Fortron 50                    Nylon

**Fig. 3-3** Single strand of Antron yarn engineered to scatter light, thus obscuring the appearance of soil. (Courtesy of E.I. du Pont de Nemours & Co., Inc., Wilmington, Delaware 19898.)

**Fig. 3-4** Heat-set yarn (shown on left) maintains fresh appearance while yarn not heat set (right) shows signs of breaking down after traffic. (Courtesy of Alexander Smith.)

To combat all these problems, the manufacturers developed second-generation yarn configurations. Since nylon had the greatest problem with static electricity, second-generation nylons such as Antron, Anso, and Cumuloft have a "conductive" material in the strands that reduces static to below normal human tolerance.

The biggest difference between first- and second-generation synthetics is in the actual shape of the individual strands of yarn. For instance, a strand of Antron III, thinner than a human hair, is not round, nor is it hairy. Its surface is smooth, and in cross section its shape is a square with rounded corners. Inside each tiny strand there are four microscopic holes running lengthwise. This "unique hollow filament structure," says Du Pont, gives a "highly effective optical light-scattering mechanism to hide the appearance of soil" and a "smooth exterior shape [which] minimizes entrapment of soil particles."

All of the second generation yarns have unusual shapes. Trevira Star polyester strands are five-pointed. Fortrel polyester is T-shaped. Herculon IV is "geometrically" shaped, according to the Hercules Corporation literature, giving flat surfaces that "reflect" light back rather than magnify soil hidden down in the carpet. Of course, all of the manufacturers claim their yarn is as good as or better than anybody else's.

Another process that has come along with synthetic yarns is "heat setting." This may be the second most important step that manufacturers

have made in recent years. Heat setting is a process whereby the yarns in your carpet are given a "permanent wave." The individual yarns are spun together and given a twist. After the twist has been put into the yarn it is run through an oven that heats the yarn until the twist is set permanently. This permanent wave tends to last and last. This gives your carpet much greater resilience than you used to get in synthetic carpets. Matting down, fuzzing out, and furniture impressions no longer need be a problem. Heat setting is the process that has made today's short shags and plushier saxonies so successful.

Another development made possible by synthetics is "solution dyeing." Here, color is introduced into the fiber during the liquid stage. This means that the color is present through the entire strand of yarn, not just on its surface (as is the case with any natural fiber and most synthetics). With a solution-dyed carpet, you can generally expect that the color will not wear off until you have actually worn the carpet down to the back. Each cleaning will refresh the color. In addition, solution-dyed yarns are highly resistant to fading by the sun.

Unfortunately, solution dyeing is only used in fibers such as Herculon IV and a few nylons. Check the label on the sample of carpet you are considering to see whether it is solution dyed.

Another advance makes the already moisture- and stain-resistant synthetics even more impregnable. In this process the fibers are coated with a chemical which resists moisture. The result is that

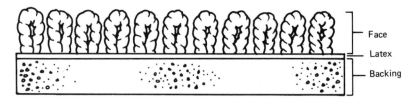

**Fig. 3-5** Cross section of foam-back carpet shows face yarn, primary back, and foam back in place of secondary jute back.

spilled liquid will "bead up" until it can be sponged off. Scotchguard, developed by 3M, is one such chemical. Another is Du Pont's Teflon.

All of these developments have made synthetics quite amazing. Today's better synthetic carpets stack up very favorably next to wool. Pound for pound they are much less expensive and more durable than wool. While wool has a feel and look all its own that no synthetic can entirely reproduce, the synthetics can now compete with regard to appearance retention, practicality, ease of maintenance, and plushness. Add their relatively low cost to this, and you can understand why there are so few wool carpets in most carpet showrooms.

Not all synthetic carpets have all of the above qualities. Many, for instance, are not treated with Scotchguard or Teflon. Most are not solution dyed. And many do not contain a specific second-generation yarn. Makers of the better carpets label their products as "practical," "durable," "easy to maintain," "easy to clean," "soil hiding," and "heat set." Reputable manufacturers stand behind these claims. The label tells you what you have a right to expect from the carpet.

**Backs**

The back of a woven carpet is an integral part of the carpet. However, even when the face yarns are synthetic, the back yarns of woven carpets are usually natural fibers such as cotton or jute. Most tufted carpets still have jute in their second back, but the primary backs are almost invariably synthetic. Increasingly, tufted carpets are being manufactured with synthetic primary and secondary backs. The Milliken Corporation's entire line is totally synthetic, featuring ActionBac, a secondary back that looks like jute but is, in fact, synthetic. Loctuft, another type of synthetic back, is usually

gray or tan and has an unwoven look, almost as though it were made of paper or cardboard. Its appearance is a drawback. Consumers seem to think it cannot be a superior back, but in my opinion it is one of the best, and very easy to work with.

A totally synthetic carpet has some very interesting properties. It is highly resistant to moisture problems such as mildew, rot, and shrinkage, which can destroy carpets made of animal or vegetable fibers. It can therefore be installed outdoors, unless the sun is going to be a problem. Here is where the fade resistance of solution-dyed yarns can be important. Combined with all-synthetic construction, solution dyeing makes for a true indoor/outdoor carpet. Basement dampness is little or no threat to totally synthetic carpets, but may soon ruin those with natural fibers in them.

Another property of totally synthetic carpets with the Action Bac or Loctuft backs is a "memory." A carpet with this property tends to return to its original shape. This generally means that it will lie flat and be much less subject to stretching and bubbling than some of the more conventionally constructed carpets.

All this does not mean that jute-backed tufted carpet, long the standard, is no good. The synthetic backs are recent innovations. The jute back is excellent and perfectly adequate for almost any normal type of installation.

Another type of secondary back is the "foam back." Here the face yarn is tufted into a primary back; then a layer of foam—either rubber or urethane, of varying thickness and density—is applied to the back. This process eliminates the need for a pad. Foam backs are usually found on less expensive residential and commercial carpets, although they are used on some very durable heavy-duty commercial grades. Foam-backed carpets are easy to install.

They do have a few limitations. Usually, the foam back does not have nearly as luxurious a feel as some might desire. Also, because foam is added, instead of a second layer of jute or other synthetic, the carpet is not nearly as strong. It will not tolerate stretching and other installation techniques that can be used when laying jute- or synthetic-backed carpets. Also, most foam-backed carpets, lacking that stronger secondary back, tend to fray at the edges and should be bound or otherwise protected. Finally, a foam-backed carpet should never be put outdoors. The foam will soak up moisture like a sponge and might take forever to dry. This might not be a serious problem for the carpet, but how would it affect a wooden floor underneath?

The foam backs tend to lie flat. The very weight of the foam (at least of a high-density rubber) back gives it this property. But foam-backed carpets sometimes stretch and bubble up in a wall-to-wall installation as the months and years go by unless they are cemented down all over.

## DURABILITY

Basically, there are four elements in the carpet construction that determine durability.

First, how much yarn has been put into the face of the carpet? This is measured by the number of ounces of yarn per square yard. In most instances you will not be able to find out how many ounces of yarn are in any particular carpet you are considering for your home, unless it is a rated commercial grade. Even the dealer cannot tell you, as manufacturers do not give these specifications for their residential lines. One exception is Bigelow, which has introduced a rating system which indicates on the sample label whether, in Bigelow's opinion, the carpet is suitable for low, medium, or heavy traffic. Reasonably close examination of a carpet sample will tell you whether it is heavier than another sample. If one sample feels heavier than another of the same size, it probably is—unless you are comparing a foam back with a jute back. The foam will weigh more.

The second durability factor is the tightness with which the yarn is woven or tufted into the carpet. The denser the weaving or tufting, the less weight each strand will have to support. Therefore, the more strands there are per square inch or square yard, the more durable the carpet will be.

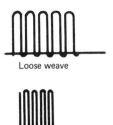

Loose weave

Tight weave

**Fig. 3-6** In a tight weave the same amount of yarn fills a smaller area than in a loose weave.

For example, suppose a manufacturer took 20 ounces of nylon and put it into a square yard of two qualities of carpet. In one quality there are eight tufts per lineal inch. In another there are twelve tufts to the inch. In the first, there will be more space between the tufts. In order to use the same amount of yarn, the individual tufts in the first square yard are higher and softer than in the second. The second square yard has strands that are shorter and more closely packed together, supporting each other. The second quality is better able to withstand traffic. In short, a tightly woven, flat-looking kitchen carpet may have the same amount of yarn as a short shag. The shag may look nicer, but the kitchen carpet will last longer.

The third basic durability factor is the type of fiber that has been put into the face of the carpet. Of today's yarn, wool is the least durable, followed by the acrylics, the polyesters, the olefins, and at the top of the list, nylon, the most durable of all. However, the polyesters and olefins are very close to nylon, and so durability may depend on which type of nylon is being compared with which type of olefin or polyester. You may find that an olefin or polyester selling at, say, $10.95 per square yard has durability comparable to the same style carpet made of nylon and selling at $10.95 per square yard. An acrylic of the same construction and price will also be comparable, but to be as durable as nylon it will definitely have more yarn per square yard in it than the others. For instance, you might find a heavy-traffic commercial carpet of nylon with 28 ounces of yarn per square yard. A polyester or olefin will have 30 or 32 ounces, but an acrylic for heavy traffic will have 40 to 48 ounces of yarn per square yard.

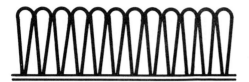

**Fig. 3-7** Level-loop weave.

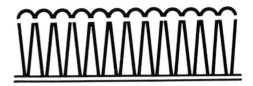

**Fig. 3-8** Tops of loops have been cut off to create "cut pile."

The fourth durability consideration is a combination of all of the elements so far discussed in this chapter. It has to do with the style and construction of the carpet. Certain types of yarn construction are necessary for certain styles of carpet but not necessary in others. Therefore, the following discussion of carpet styles will include those elements of yarn construction that will be important to you.

## CARPET STYLES

Most of the styles of carpet being offered by the literally hundreds of mills can be broken down into types.

### Level Loop

The most common is the level loop. A level loop is exactly that. It is a carpet constructed with loops, all of which are the same height. Most kitchen and commercial carpets from the least to the most expensive are of this type. Level-loop carpets are practical because they are quite durable and easy to clean. With the loop weave, you walk on the sides of the yarn strands rather than on the ends. Because the yarn is held securely in a rather tight weave, it is much less likely that individual strands of yarn will fuzz than in some residential styles of carpet. The tighter the construction—the more stitches or tufts per square inch—the more durable and easy to clean the carpet will be.

If you examine the individual yarns in level-loop carpets, you will usually find that they do not have much of a twist, and there is no indication on the label that the yarn has been heat set. This is because the very construction of the carpet makes these features unnecessary. The carpet is so tightly woven that the texture is not soft enough to require resiliency.

If a level-loop carpet is very loosely woven, there should be a twist on the yarns, and you should check the label to see if it is heat set. Loosely woven level-loop carpets are usually intended for residential use, and have a much deeper pile and softer feel. You will have to determine whether or not you think these qualities are important in the carpet you are examining.

One possible problem can arise with any level-loop carpet. If the loop gets pulled out for some reason, it can result in an entire row of yarn being pulled out. This is because in level-loop carpets the yarn is inserted in one continuous thread. When the yarn is pulled out it leaves an ugly bare line in the carpet. This can be a real problem along the edges and where seams occur. The mills are very much aware of this potential problem and, in their better commercial grades, many of them feature a high "tuft bind." This refers to how much strength it takes to pull a loop or tuft out of the carpet. This should not be as much of a problem in a residence as in some commercial installations, but you certainly should be aware of the possiblity of loops pulling out and methods you can use to prevent it (see Chapters 7 and 8).

Finally, keep in mind that while there are many very inexpensive kitchen and indoor/outdoor level-loop carpets on the market, the cheaper they are the more they sacrifice—usually the amount of yarn per square yard tufted into the goods. Some seemingly very tightly woven fabrics have only 10 ounces of yarn per square yard.

### Cut Pile

Cut-pile carpet is level-loop carpet with the tops of the loops shaved off. Here, the density of the yarn can be very important to you. The tighter the weave the more durable it is likely to be. If you combine a dense weave with a deep pile it will be

Random sheared

**Fig. 3-9** Cutting some, but not all, tops of loops creates a "random" or "tip-sheared" effect.

**Fig. 3-10** The classic "velvet" effect is shown in Bigelow's "Katsura." Notice shading or highlighting creating a two-tone effect. (Courtesy Bigelow-Sanford Inc.)

yet more durable (more yarn per square yard), and if you add to this a tight, heat-set twist, you will have a carpet that is very practical and feels and looks elegant.

Here again, the twist and heat set are not always necessary. You will often find carpets, especially acrylics, that are designed to look like the traditional wool plushes and are not heat set. These should also be quite tightly woven so that the individual strands of yarn have a much better chance of supporting each other.

## Random or Tip Sheared

Tip-sheared or random-sheared carpet is a combination of level loop and the cut pile. The manufac-

turer has sheared some but not all of the tops of the loops. This strikes a compromise between the practicality of the level loop and the elegance of the cut pile. All we have said about the cut pile applies here. Unless the carpet is very densely tufted or woven it should, in my opinion, be heat set.

## Velvet

A real velvet carpet has a special weave made on a velvet loom. Many people in the industry refer to cut-pile carpets as "velvet," and many cut-pile carpets look like the traditional velvet fabrics used for upholstery or clothing. One aspect of velvet and/or most cut-pile carpets is that they have a definite

**Fig. 3-11** Masland's "Rivoli" combines level loop with cut pile to create "tip-sheared" effect, then runs lower-level loop to create pronounced "carved" effect. (Courtesy C.H. Masland and Sons.)

tendency toward "shading," or "highlighting." In a cut-pile carpet, all of the threads in the face are standing up. You walk on their ends. How this carpet looks to you depends entirely on how it reflects the light in the room. If all of the strands of yarn really did stand perfectly straight, the carpet would appear to be a flat monotone. This effect is impossible because as soon as you walk on, vacuum, or in any way disturb the face of the carpet, the strands fall into enough disarray so that the light reflects off the sides of the yarn in various ways. This is why footprints show, and why your vacuum cleaner leaves tracks. Some carpets have a finer surface finish than others, and so produce more shading. Shading in cut-pile carpet is to some extent unavoidable. This is not a manufacturing

defect. To the connoisseur, it may even be a sign of elegance.

**Sculptured or Carved**

Carpets can be sculptured or carved into a variety of designs. A sculptured or carved carpet is basically a carpet with two or more levels to it. It may be a cut-pile or velvet carpet with a line of loops running through it at a lower level, giving a carved effect. It may be a loop weave with two or more levels to the loops, giving it a more interesting texture. A number of tightly woven commercial grades are made this way; they have most of the practical advantages of the plain level loop but look a little nicer. Some velvet or cut-pile carpets have

**Fig. 3-12** Masland's "Centennial" illustrates one of the more loosely woven short shags. (Courtesy C.H. Masland and Sons.)

actually been carved—that is, the yarn has been cut or carved out of the face either by machine or by hand. One possible disadvantage is that dirt and crumbs tend to get lodged in the grooves. A proper vacuum cleaner (see Chapter 12) should be able to overcome this problem.

### Shag or Short Shag

These are the very loosely woven or tufted carpets where the yarn tends to be very floppy. Most of the longer shags have left the market because they tended to mat down. The yarns were so long that there was no way they could be made to stand up over any period of time. The shorter shags, however, are still very popular. The new heat-setting techniques add to their resiliency, making them very satisfactory for many applications. Given the right type of vacuum cleaner and a light to medium traffic situation, a loosely woven short shag with as few as 24 ounces of yarn per square yard can be perfectly adequate for certain residential situations. One possible advantage of the short shag is a result of its loose weave. The fact that you can see down to the back of the carpet—so much so

32 Types of Carpet and Padding

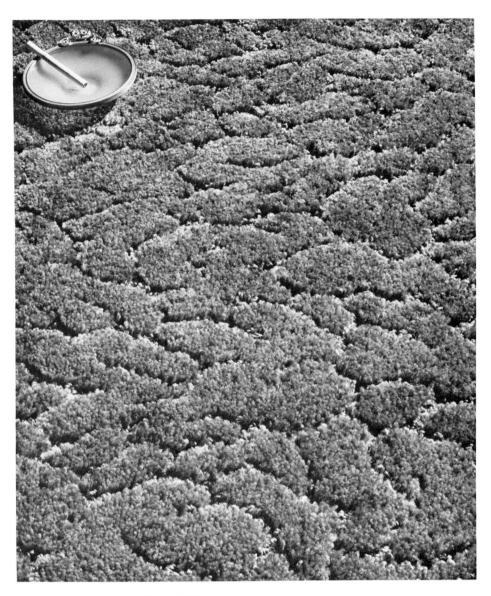

**Fig. 3-13** "Breckenwood" by Milliken shows a sculptured shag (also called a cut and loop). (Courtesy Milliken Carpets.)

that some mills color the back—means that your vacuum cleaner can also "see" the back, and dirt does not get lodged down there with regular cleaning.

**Cut and Loop or Sculptured Shag**

This is exactly what the name implies—a shag or cut pile (usually short) that has a design running through it at a lower height, usually a loop weave. Some of these styles are constructed so that the loop not only runs in a distinct line, creating a

pattern in the goods, but is also intermingled with the shag portion as in a tip-sheared carpet. However, with the cut-and-loop or sculptured shag, the loop usually is lower in height than the shag and not visible until you pull the individual threads of the shag apart and look down into the pile. The presence of this loop mixed in with the shag adds to the carpet's resiliency, making it unlikely to mat down and lie flat. Here heat setting is most important. Of course, the heavier the shag (the more yarn per square yard) and the tighter its weave, the greater its durability. This leads us to the next three styles.

**Fig. 3-14** "Bali Hai II," Masland's cut pile, illustrates densely tufted saxony with definite heat-set twist in the yarn. (Courtesy C.H. Masland and Sons.)

### Plush

The plush carpet is actually a heavy-cut pile. It is normally quite deep, and tightly woven.

### Splush

And the "splush" is somewhere between the shag and the plush. It's a compromise. When does a shag become a splush and a splush a plush? I don't think anybody knows. You will have to be the judge. In any case, with all of these heat setting is

very important, unless you are dealing with one of the very tightly woven or tufted plushes.

### Saxony

The saxony has pretty much taken over where the term *splush* used to apply. It is a carpet of medium-height (such as a short shag) cut pile that has a definite twist on the yarn and is most certainly heat set. It is usually heavier than the short shag (although there are plenty of so-called saxonies which I would call short shags) and it can be found

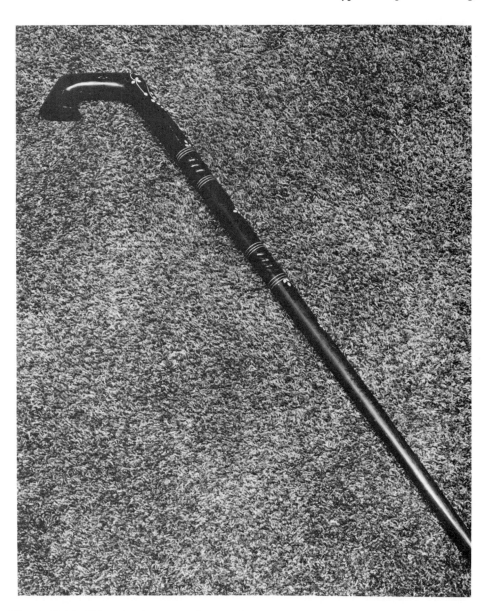

**Fig. 3-15** Traditional twist weave is seen in Milliken's "Grand Tradition." (Courtesy Milliken Carpets.)

in very heavy, tightly woven fabrics. I know of one with 80 ounces of yarn per square yard and a pile height of about ⅝ of an inch. The leading characteristics of the saxony are the heat-set twist in the yarn and the cut, single-level pile. The saxony is undoubtedly the most popular style carpet on the market as of this writing.

## Twist or Frieze

The twist weave is not nearly as common as it used to be, due to the development of heat setting and

the appearance of the more elegant-looking saxonies. The twist is made with yarn that has had a very high degree of twist put into it, so tight that it looks like a strand of tightly twisted cotton string. The individual threads woven into the carpet are not very long—usually somewhere between ¼ and ½ of an inch—and they tend to be a bit shaggy or tangled up with each other. The twist is normally quite tightly woven or tufted so that it is difficult to see the back. Most twists are quite durable and practical. Some are rated for commercial traffic. To be sure of a twist's overall resilience you should

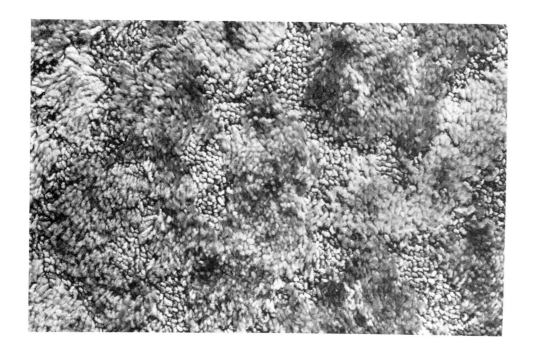

**Fig. 3-16b** Same basic cut-and-loop construction gives entirely different effects in these illustrations. Milliken's "Pattern 1550" (top) uses a heavy concentration of loop pile with higher cut pile for pronounced cut-and-loop design. Bigelow's "Hawaiian Vista" uses more subtle, hardly noticeable, loop weave running through cut pile for softer, less rugged appearance. (Courtesy Milliken Carpets and Bigelow-Sanford Inc.)

make sure it has been heat set, even though this was not done in the past.

## Needlebond

Needlebonded carpet is the original indoor/outdoor carpet first brought out by Ozite in the 1960s. This carpet looks like felt to many people. It is quite flat, with no pile to it. It is totally synthetic, and certainly stands up to moisture. Some better grades use solution-dyed yarns and do not fade easily. Most are relatively inexpensive and quite durable. They are durable almost entirely because of their thickness, although one made of acrylic will not last as long as one the same thickness made of nylon. Most needlebonded carpets are available with or without a foam back. As with a foam-backed level loop, one has to question whether foam-back needlebonded carpet is suitable for outdoors, where moisture might damage a subfloor. Keeping the cheaper grades looking clean, especially the lighter colors, can be a problem.

## Mixtures

Finally, we have all the variations on all of the previously discussed styles. With tufting and synthetics, almost anything is possible, but most carpets you look at will be one or more of the styles just described. Just as the sculptured shag is a combination of the sculptured concept and the shag, a twist can be mixed in with a saxony, and so on. Colored needlebonded carpet can be used as a primary back for a short shag. The mill will use a green back to go with a green face yarn, making the short shag look a bit better.

## PADDING

Padding can be made from both natural and synthetic materials. The natural materials are hair, jute, "cotton or whatever," and rubber. The all-hair pad is often made of horsehair. It is a very firm pad compared to some of the more popular pads today. It is also quite expensive. Therefore, most firm pads are a mixture of hair and jute. Jute is not nearly as resilient a fiber as hair, so the more jute there is in a hair and jute pad, the less resilient it will be overall. Fiber pads, especially those with a lot of jute, tend to break down in a shorter period

There are three types of carpet installations:

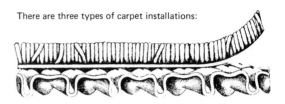

1. Carpet installed over separate cushion.

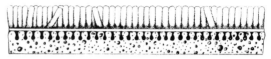

2. Carpet with attached cushioning.

3. Direct glue down: Carpet cemented directly to floor without any cushioning.

**Fig. 3-17** Three types of carpet installation are shown above. (Courtesy Carpet Cushion Council.)

of time than some of the better sponge-type pads. If you put a fiber pad under an area rug such as an oriental, you probably will have to replace it from time to time. Hair-and-jute pads are often rubberized on the top and bottom with a thin layer of latex to help prevent deterioration.

The "cotton or whatever" classification is my own. There are a number of fiber pads on the market today that look very much like hair or hair-and-jute pads. But they are made up of miscellaneous surplus fibers that the manufacturer has blended to create the pad. "Cotton or whatever" pads usually contain a certain amount of hair and jute along with everything else. Generally speaking, they can be expected to behave the same as hair-and-jute pads.

All fiber pads tend to be quite firm. They do not add softness or plushness to the carpet the way that the more popular sponge-type pads might. However, this fact may be to your advantage in certain situations. Certain woven carpets require fiber pads. Many woven carpets have very stiff backs—almost impossible to stretch while being installed (see Chapter 9). Yet, if the back of the carpet is subjected to constant flexing over the months and years it will loosen up and stretch on its own. If the carpet has been installed wall to wall

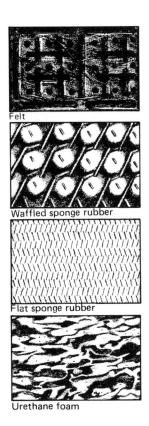

Felt

Waffled sponge rubber

Flat sponge rubber

Urethane foam

**Fig. 3-18** Felt (hair-and-jute), waffle, sponge-rubber, and urethane-foam pads are illustrated above. (Courtesy Carpet Cushion Council.)

and it begins to stretch, it has no place to go except up—in the form of bubbles. The use of a firm pad cuts down the amount of flexing dramatically and helps to prevent this problem.

Another reason to choose a firmer pad is that it may give greater protection to your carpet than one of the spongier types. There is a certain amount of controversy over this question in the carpet industry today. The theory behind padding is that the pad helps insulate the carpet from the floor when a foot or other object strikes it. The pad cushions the blow. There is no doubt that a good quality hair or hair-and-jute pad accomplishes this, whereas some of the spongier pads offer practically no resistance to the blow—the foot goes directly to the floor, right through the plush softness.

Under area rugs, the spongier pads tend to cause a certain amount of movement due to the constant flexing of the back of the rug. Where a carpet has been stretched in properly wall to wall this should not be a problem. But with an area rug,

especially a floppy-type oriental, a spongy pad can create a problem.

Another kind of natural pad is rubber. Rubber pads are made in a fairly firm sponge type and a plushier "waffle" type. The sponge is normally about ¼ to ⅜ of an inch thick. It is quite dense, and makes an excellent compromise between the very firm hair pad and the very soft rubber or synthetic pad. The waffle type has a supposed "thickness" of as much as ½ of an inch or more, but most of this is in the form of air. The actual thickness of the rubber may be as little as ¹/₁₆ of an inch. There usually is some sort of webbing on the back to give strength to the pad.

All of the types of padding discussed thus far are rated according to the number of ounces per square yard they weigh. The more ounces the better. The 32-ounce hair-and-jute pad should be a minimum, but there are lighter weights around. A 40-ounce pad is standard and quite adequate for most needs. Heavier weights give a somewhat softer and plushier feel to the carpet and are quite thick, but firm.

Rubber pads should weigh 60 ounces per square yard, and 64 would be better. An 80-ounce waffle-type pad gives a real sense of elegance and a great deal more protection to the carpet.

Rubber pads lead us into the synthetics as many of the rubbers actually are, to a large extent if not totally, synthetic. It is hard to know which they are and it really does not matter that much. One of the elements in rubber padding is clay. Some pads have more clay than others. This is why some of these pads dry out and disintegrate over the years. It is almost impossible for you to know whether a pad has more clay than it should. The only precaution you can take is to seek assurance from the dealer that the pad will last for the life of the carpet being installed over it. The dealer should be able to guarantee this, and many padding manufacturers will as well.

Most synthetic pads on the market today are made of polyurethane foam and are commonly called *prime* or *rebonded* urethane. Prime urethane pads all look pretty much the same in consistency, although they come in an amazing variety of colors. But looks have very little to do with their quality. They come in varying thicknesses from ¼ up to ¾ of an inch. But even thickness is not all there is to consider. The major element to consider is the pad's density. The more dense a urethane pad is the more firm it will be.

Rebonded urethane is prime urethane that has been "chewed up" mechanically and then put back together in a much heavier and denser composition. This product, unlike prime urethane, has a tendency to crumble when handled, although like prime urethane it tears easily when handled. Neither of these problems occurs once the pads are under the carpet. They should perform adequately as long as they are guaranteed to last for the life of your carpet.

It is my opinion that the firmer urethane pads (just as with the rubber and fiber pads) give your carpet better protection. The more the carpet is protected from your foot going to the floor the better. Probably the best test for the quality of pad suitable for your purposes is one you can conduct. Simply take a sample of the carpet you have chosen and put it on top of each of the pads you are considering, then walk on it. The pad that gives you the feel you want is the one you ought to buy.

Some manufacturers have introduced such terms as *initial load deflection* or *indent load deflection* which they claim describe what you should be looking for better than the term *density*. What they are saying is that the thickness or weight of the pad does not mean as much as the actual performance of the pad under your foot. Initial load deflection relates to the extent to which the pad lets your foot go all the way to the floor after it has given your foot an initial sense of plushness.

Pads that give a firmer feel and keep your foot from going directly to the floor cost more than softer pads. The pad industry is possibly more highly competitive than the carpet industry, so there are always new, unbelievably light (practically all air) pads being introduced at lower prices. These pads certainly do give an initial sense of plushness, and seem to many people to be exactly the feel they want. As long as the manufacturer guarantees that the pad will not lose its thickness (will not "bottom out" or deteriorate) during the life of the carpet, this may be all you need. The life of the carpet may well be enhanced by a better pad, but today's better synthetic carpets are so amazingly durable and easy to maintain that you might decide anything the pad may add to its life will be marginal. Another consideration is the length of time you plan to use the carpet.

## POSSIBLE PITFALLS

Most of the problems that arise with floor covering show up within one year after installation, and will be taken care of by any reputable dealer and manufacturer. You should be aware of what can happen, and be able to distinguish between real problems and matters that can be taken care of easily.

Your wall-to-wall carpet might bubble up in places after a few months of use. This means the carpet needs restretching. If you installed it, then you will have to restretch it (see Chapter 9). If not, whoever installed the product for you will restretch it. In short, this is usually an installation problem, not a manufacturing problem, and is the responsibility of the installer. One possible exception is where there actually is a manufacturing defect having to do with improper application of latex adhesive in the carpet back. I did see one installation where no amount of stretching solved the problem. The carpet seemed to have an infinite amount of stretch in it. The mill agreed, and replaced the carpet for the consumer.

Another problem is shedding. This means that every time you vacuum the carpet you fill the vacuum bag with an alarming amount of yarn from the carpet. Generally speaking, this is normal with cut-pile carpet and even with some loop weaves. Most new carpets shed to some extent. This is not a defect; yarn that has been fastened into the back of the carpet is not coming out. Shedding almost always diminishes over the months, although I have seen carpets that never seem to stop shedding. My own living room carpet, which has been down for five years, still sheds a certain amount when vacuumed.

A related problem is "pilling." Pilling is where the carpet sheds but the shed fibers refuse to leave the carpet. Instead, they cling to the surface and ball up. Sometimes it takes quite a bit of strength to pull these balls off the carpet. This is more common in certain level-loop and tip-sheared carpets than in today's heat-set, cut-pile carpets. You should not have to put up with pilling in any of today's carpets made of second-generation yarns. If it does occur, complain to your dealer. Most dealers and manufacturers will replace carpets that do not perform as described on labels and in advertising.

Sometimes a highly competitive situation can bring about unethical practices among sales organizations. The following examples which have been observed in the floor-covering industry are unusual, but you should be aware that they can occur.

Mills quite frequently bring out a particular style of carpet in two or more grades. These might be rated by the mill as "good," "better," and "best." The three grades may be of the same basic construction, the same yarn, and the same color, but there will be more yarn per square yard and tighter construction as you proceed from good to better to best. Sometimes it is difficult to tell the difference between good and better or better and best after they have been installed. Unscrupulous salesmen have been known to make a switch. They may show the customer the better grade, not revealing that there is a good grade, and then install the good. This practice might explain a particularly low price.

There are ways to prevent this from happening to you. The most obvious method is to know who you are dealing with. Most dealers have a reputation to maintain and will not risk spoiling it with such a practice. But if you suspect that something like this is happening to you, make a comparison between a sample of the carpet you have chosen and the actual carpet going in. You should also ask to see the label on the wrapper taken from your carpet. If the carpet is not a stock item cut off a roll in the dealer's warehouse but rather a special cut ordered from the mill or a local wholesale distributor, the wrapping will have a "sidemark" on it, giving the pattern number, color, and the size of the cut. This will coincide exactly with what you ordered, with the possible exception of the size. The size might be different because sometimes the dealer will order a particular size cut for you only to find that the warehouse has a piece sitting on the shelf which is a little bigger than needed. The dealer may take this "balance" from the distributor, having made arrangements to pay no more for the carpet than he would have if the distributor had sent exactly the correct amount.

Another dishonest practice is that of telling the unsuspecting customer that he/she needs more floor covering than is actually required. This allows the dealer to charge less per square yard because fewer square yards will actually go onto the floor than "estimated." The customer will be impressed by the resulting low bid. If you have read Chapter 1, this will not happen to you.

Finally, there's the "I can get it for you wholesale" syndrome. If somebody can get it for you wholesale, make sure you know who they are, where they are located, and whether they will be around next year to take care of any problems that might arise. Service is a large part of the floor-covering business. Selling the floor to you can be only the beginning. The reputable dealer is there to take care of any problems that might arise with regard to the quality of the goods. This is worth something, and if you have a problem, it can be worth a great deal.

The finished product. Here a wall to wall installation of Bigelow's "Sahara Sands" combines with contemporary furnishings to produce elegant overall effect. (Courtesy Bigelow-Sanford, Inc.)

Most any effect is possible with today's carpet patterns. Milliken's "Pattern 1690 Plaid" gives elegant but casual effect in a dining and recreation room setting. (Courtesy Milliken Carpets.)

Here real imagination creates a dramatic effect by combining 2 carpet styles in the same room (Milliken's "Sun Mist" and "Sun Isle"). (Courtesy Milliken Carpets.)

# 4 Types of Linoleum and Tile

Today most linoleums and tiles are made with vinyl. Some are solid vinyl, some partly vinyl. This synthetic has introduced a whole new era of amazingly durable and easy-to-maintain floors.

## HOW IS LINOLEUM MADE?

Linoleum is: "a floor covering formed by coating burlap or canvas with linseed oil, powdered cork, and rosin. Pigments are added to create the desired colors and patterns." This definition is from the *American College Dictionary* of 1948. With very few exceptions, this technical definition does not apply today. The word *linoleum* has come to mean any of the synthetic floors which have replaced the more traditional product.

Most of these floors are either inlaid or rotogravure. Inlaid means that the pattern or color of the product extends through the product from the top surface to the back of the goods. Its durability depends on how thick the pattern is. A ⅛-inch-thick pattern is twice as durable as a ¹/₁₆-inch-thick pattern. The pattern lasts as long as the thickness lasts. No matter how much you wear off the surface, the pattern will remain until it is worn to the back.

Inlaid linoleums (inlaids) tend to be quite stiff and difficult to handle. They are normally avail-

able only 6 feet wide and are usually installed by the "pattern scribing" method (see Chapter 10).

Armstrong is a major supplier of inlaid vinyl today. Another is NAFCO. A few inlaid vinyls (such as Congoleum's Fashionflor and Reflections II) are available from other mills. But the other mills primarily manufacture rotogravure floor coverings. These are much softer and easier to handle. Hence, many come 9, 12, and even 15 feet wide.

Rotogravure is a printing process used in the manufacture of magazines and newspapers. It has been adapted to the manufacture of vinyls so that today almost any pattern imaginable can be created for use on your floor. The term *printing* with regard to floor covering often conjures up an image of inferior durability, but this should not be the case. Some of the most durable products available are rotogravure, lasting as long as twenty years or more.

Rotogravure floor coverings are durable because a clear vinyl wear layer has been added to the surface. This transparent wear layer protects the pattern, so the thickness of the wear layer determines how long the product will last. A rule of thumb in the industry is that you can expect about one year of wear for every thousandth of an inch of wear layer. A product with 5 thousandths of an inch of clear vinyl should last about five years. One

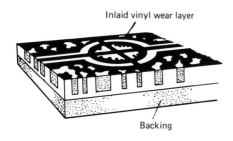

**Fig. 4-1** Inlaid linoleum. Note pattern going through from top to back.

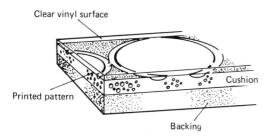

**Fig. 4-2** Rotogravure linoleum. Note clear vinyl surface covers printed pattern. Cushion is sandwiched between pattern and back for cushioned effect.

with 20 thousandths should last around twenty years. Manufacturers cannot guarantee such performance because they have no control over how much traffic the product will be subjected to. Nevertheless, comparing product specifications with this rule of thumb should give you an excellent idea of what performance you can expect.

## NO-WAX FEATURES

The no-wax linoleums were introduced with the advent of rotogravure products with the clear vinyl wear layer. Congoleum coined the phrase *shinyl vinyl.* It is true that these surfaces are very easy to maintain. They are nonporous and highly, though not totally, stain resistant. You do need to read manufacturers' maintenance recommendations very carefully before you accept the no-wax description as totally accurate. Mills generally recommend that you use their "dressing" on their rotogravure floors (unless they have added a coating of polyurethane to the surface—more

about this shortly). This dressing is applied with a damp mop in the same manner as many acrylic floor finishes on the market.

One of GAF's technical manuals states: "If heavy wear dulls the surface, the gloss may be restored and maintained by mechanical buffing with a lamb's wool pad." In other words, you can buff your floor dry with a buffing machine using a lamb's wool pad. The friction will help eliminate any film you have not been able to remove by regular cleaning, and according to one mill representative from GAF, buffing will "recure the clear vinyl wear layer." Congoleum literature recommends the same procedure. I have not been able to get an Armstrong representative to say directly to me that the same is true for their rotogravure products. Yet Armstrong representatives agree that their rotogravure floors have basically the same clear vinyl wear layer. In any case, the recommendation to buff these floors dry certainly suggests that they require no wax.

Many inlaid vinyl floors require waxing or application of some sort of proper dressing (see Chapter 12). Armstrong has responded to the no-wax competition by adding a clear polyurethane wear layer to the surface of many of their products. For as long as this polyurethane wear layer lasts (Armstrong calls it Mirabond) no wax or dressing of any kind need be applied. The floor will maintain its shine as long as it is kept clean. However, according to Armstrong, the Mirabond finish can only be expected to last three to five years. Thereafter it has to be maintained by the home owner with Armstrong's Suncoat Floor Finish.

The polyurethane wear layer is an amazingly easy surface to maintain. Armstrong has had such tremendous success with the Solarian line of Mirabond finished products that the other mills have added a polyurethane wear layer to some of their rotogravure products. Here you get the clear vinyl wear layer plus the high-shine urethane finish—perhaps the best of both worlds. As with Armstrong's Mirabond, the urethane finishes wear off after a certain number of years and have to be maintained periodically using each manufacturer's recommended product. Of course, you may find the somewhat duller shine of the clear vinyl perfectly satisfactory and decide you don't need to restore the original high shine.

## CUSHIONED FLOORS

The development of the rotogravure process also brought about the development of the cushioned vinyls. Most of these vinyls have a cushion or foam layer sandwiched between the pattern and the back. Some of these cushions are practically imperceptible, but others are quite thick and can give a relatively soft feel underfoot, especially when compared to the inlaid linoleums. And, while the inlaid linoleums tend to be very stiff and difficult to handle, many of the good quality cushioned products are pliable and almost as easy to work with as foam-backed carpet.

Armstrong is now producing cushioned floors that are designed primarily for the do-it-yourselfer. These Interflex floors are made with polyvinyl chloride (PVC) from top to bottom, except where the Mirabond urethane wear layer has been added. The 100 percent PVC construction makes these products so pliable that they can take incredible abuse in handling. While many other rotogravure products on the market are relatively easy to work with and perfectly suitable for the do-it-yourselfer, their non-PVC backs do tend to be more easily damaged when being worked into position prior to trimming-in and cementing.

In addition, Armstrong's 100 percent PVC floors require fastening at the edges and seams only (see Chapter 10). They will not bubble up later because of stretching, as will most floors if they are not cemented all over. Because they do not require cementing all over, they require much less floor preparation than other products do (See Chapter 6). It should be mentioned, however, that you must pay very careful attention to securely fastening seams and edges of these floors exactly as Armstrong directs.

## SEAMLESS FLOORS

Most linoleums are made 6 feet wide. Therefore, except for very small rooms, most installations require seams—and seams in linoleum have been a source of aggravation for the home owner for as long as the product has been in existence. Seams can part, curl, break at the edges, and so forth.

The mills are fully aware of these problems and have worked out all sorts of remedies. To prevent curling, for instance, they have special "contact" adhesives to be used under the seams and around the edges of materials that have such a tendency. The backs have been improved to prevent shrinkage and parting at the seams. Most of the rotogravure products are now supposed to be installed with a special seam sealer that "welds" the two edges of the seam together, giving a "seamless" installation. NAFCO has developed a seam-sealing method for their solid vinyl inlaid. Most of these remedies work most of the time, but not all of the time.

Therefore, the manufacturers have tried to create truly seamless products, that is, floors that go into a room in one piece. To do this they have produced their easier-to-handle rotogravure products in even wider versions. They started with 6-foot goods, then went to 9 feet, then 12, and now Congoleum's Spring is available 15 feet wide. As long as one of the dimensions of your room is less than one of these widths you can have a seamless floor. But this can involve a tremendous amount of waste and just might not be worth it.

Another way to get a seamless installation is to purchase a "poured floor." The poured floor is literally manufactured right on the job. The installer brings all of the chemicals, including the pigments, to your home in liquid or powder form and makes the floor in place. A poured floor, properly installed, is usually very satisfactory and quite durable. However, the chemicals are highly volatile while in their liquid state. They also are extremely toxic and dangerous to inhale. They only should be installed by a highly qualified and experienced person. Also, they are very limited in color and pattern and tend to be very expensive.

## TILE

Unlike most carpet tiles, linoleum (called *resilient* in the trade) tiles come in a wide variety of styles and patterns, and range in price from very cheap to extremely expensive. Compared to linoleum roll (sometimes called *sheet*) goods, tile floors are relatively easy to install—especially some of the peel-and-stick varieties currently on the market.

Most floor tiles are made of either rubber, asphalt, vinyl asbestos (VA) or solid vinyl. Rubber tile has practically left the market, although there are a few grades available. Asphalt tile is not nearly as prevalent as it was before the vinyls entered the market. Depending on thickness, both rubber and asphalt tile tend to be very durable. Asphalt is quite inexpensive. Neither of these floors is as easy to maintain as the vinyls.

The most popular tile today is vinyl asbestos. Many of these tiles are inlaid. As long as the tile lasts, the pattern lasts. But be careful—many of the patterns have been printed onto surfaces that have an inlaid marbleized effect. While the marbleized effect will last until the tile is worn down to the back, the pattern may wear off.

Most residential VA tiles are made $^1/_{16}$ of an inch thick. Some are available $^3/_{32}$ of an inch and some ⅛ of an inch. The last is usually considered necessary for commercial installations.

Except for some of the fancier patterns, residential VA tile is about the least expensive floor available. It also is quite satisfactory in most installations, as far as durability is concerned. But it usually does need to be dressed to keep it easy to clean.

VA tile also tends to be quite hard underfoot, and brittle. It can break up if installed over a bouncy subfloor.

Solid vinyl tile is considerably more expensive than VA, although there are some exceptions. It is much more pliable than VA, and less likely to break up. The better grades can also be expected to last much longer. It is in the very fine solid vinyl tiles that you find incredibly real-looking reproductions of such surfaces as stone, slate, brick, quarry tile, and ceramic tile. (Some of the VA tile and rotogravure sheet-goods manufacturers are making great strides in this direction too.) Solid vinyl tiles may require a dressing, but there are some no-wax VA and solid vinyl tiles that have a coat of polyurethane on the surface.

To make tile truly a do-it-yourself product, the manufacturers have added a coat of adhesive to the backs of many of their patterns. This eliminates the need to spread adhesive prior to laying the tile. Be very certain the floor is absolutely dust-free before installing "peel-and-stick" resilient and carpet tiles (see Chapter 11). Adhesive-backed tile is a relatively easy floor to install.

The one major drawback to tile is also its advantage. It is installed one 9-inch by 9-inch (or

12-inch by 12-inch) tile at a time. A mistake in trimming ruins only one tile, not an entire floor. The disadvantage is that you have a seam every 9 or 12 inches, depending on the size of the tiles. As yet, no manufacturer has come out with a seam-sealing method for tile. There is no such thing as a seamless tile floor.

## POSSIBLE PITFALLS

Generally speaking, you will find that your linoleum or tile will perform exactly as it is supposed to, as long as you follow the manufacturer's specifications regarding maintenance (see Chapter 12). For example, no-wax surfaces really are incredibly trouble-free, but you must not abuse your floor, expecting it to be impervious to any and all treatment. A no-wax floor has to be kept clean; dirt and grit will destroy the surface. You must protect it from sharp edges on appliances and from chair and table legs which may leave indentations or cut the floor. And you must not expect your floor to be immune to cigarette burns. Damages from these causes are not covered by guarantees or warrantees from the dealer or manufacturer.

You may have a legitimate claim if seams do not stay down, or linoleum bubbles in the center or curls at the edges. There may be a failure in the adhesive or seam sealer. Or you may find that the wear layer is peeling off your rotogravure floor. This is known as "delamination," and normally is considered a manufacturing defect.

The best way to avoid problems is to be sure you follow all of the manufacturer's recommendations. This is especially true if you are installing the floor yourself. If the dealer installs the floor, then any installation problems are the dealer's. But if you install it, the problems are yours.

One great way for the manufacturers to get around honoring a complaint is to tell you that you used the wrong underlayment board, or the wrong flooring felt, or the wrong adhesive. You might have used Armstrong's flooring felt under Congoleum's linoleum and cemented the whole thing with GAF's adhesive. The professionals do this all the time, but if you are taking on the responsibility of the installation, be sure the manufacturer of the tile or linoleum will not object to any of the materials you may use.

# 5 What Are the Costs and Risks of Doing It Yourself?

As you will see, there is no mystique to floor-covering installation. Most of it is a question of common sense and practice. But if this is your first try, you may want to determine whether the money saved by doing it yourself will outweigh the risks.

## POSSIBLE SAVINGS

Labor costs for most floor-covering installations are figured by either the square yard or the square foot. Most jobs involving broadloom carpet or linoleum sheet goods are figured by the square yard; most tile jobs by the square foot. Subfloor preparation prior to installation of the new floor is normally figured separately. Usually underlayment-board installation is figured by the square foot or by the 4-by-4 or 4-by-8-foot sheet.

Rates for installation vary greatly from one region of the country to another. Even within one region there can be a wide range of prices for the same service, depending on how experienced, how good, and how "hungry" the installer may be.

Another cost factor is the size and difficulty of the job. A large house with no furniture in it may command a lower price per square yard than a single room loaded with furniture.

You should check with several dealers and find out how much they charge for your type of installation. Keep in mind that there may be extra charges for such things as stairs, metal strips required in doorways, seams, moving furniture (especially appliances), trimming doors, and so forth.

Once you know the prevailing rates you can employ some simple arithmetic to determine how much the professionals are going to charge to install your floor covering. After you have read Chapter 1 on measuring, you will be able to figure how much material you need. That figure multiplied by the rate per square yard or foot for labor in your area, plus charges for any extras, should give you a pretty good idea of how much you will have to pay to have a professional do it.

Next to this total you will need to balance the cost of your time, unless, as with many do-it-yourselfers, this factor is not important to you. You should probably figure that it will take you twice as long to do it as a professional, since you will have a lot of sorting out to do along the way to make sure you are getting it right. Don't forget to add the cost of supplies (normally included in the professional's rate). Supplies may include tackless stripping, staples, adhesives, seaming tape, door metal, tools, and cutting blades. Add all these together, subtract them from what the professional would charge, and the final figure is the net savings.

This type of figuring can be done for carpet, linoleum, or tile. Usually it takes longer to install linoleum than carpet, a fact that is reflected in the installer's price. While the price for installing tile is estimated by the square foot instead of the square yard, the same type of figuring applies.

## POSSIBLE RISKS

There is one important factor which has not been added into the above figures. Suppose you do it yourself and you damage the goods?

If someone makes a mistake in figuring or installation, correction is that person's responsibility. If the do-it-yourselfer makes the mistake, it is his/her problem. If the professional makes the mistake, it is his/her problem. If the professional is working for a dealer, then he/she is acting on behalf of the dealer and it becomes the dealer's problem.

It is, therefore, very important for you to carefully study your situation and try to determine the chances that you might damage the material to an extent that requires purchasing a whole new piece. This usually depnds on the kind of material you are working with.

Tile, for instance, (carpet, VA, or vinyl) is relatively easy to work with. If you make a mistake in cutting one of the tiles, you have damaged only one tile. If you did not order enough material you'll probably be able to order more with few problems other than a delay in finishing the job.

Foam-backed shag or sculptured shag carpet does not generally show mistakes. If you cut the carpet wrong or even tear it, chances are you'll be able to put it back together leaving no trace of the problem. If you have ordered too little, you may well be able to purchase more and put the whole thing together with little difficulty. The problem with purchasing more is that you might not be able to get the same dye lot. This means that the roll from which your first cut came might have been dyed at a different time from the roll from which your second cut came. While the two are ostensibly the same color, it is impossible for the dealer to guarantee that you will have a perfect color match. An alternative to buying more is to fill in your shortage using waste you had planned to throw away or install in a closet. In any case, with

foam-backed or sculptured shag carpets there usually are ways of solving the problem. The following chapters on installation will make many solutions seem much less difficult than they might as you read this paragraph.

Foam-backed carpet of the level-loop variety does not have as much depth of pile to work with as shag. It is not quite as "forgiving" as shag, but it is still quite easy to work with and repair. It just requires that you be a bit more meticulous when fixing bad cuts and tears.

If your carpet is being installed with tackless stripping over a pad, the same difficulties may arise as with foam-back carpets. However, repairs can be made; the professionals run into these problems more frequently than they like to admit, and take care of them without the customer ever knowing it. Chances are you can conceal your mistakes as well.

None of the linoleums is as easy to work with and repair as foam-backed shag or even level-loop carpets. But many of the rotogravure products and the new do-it-yourself linoleums from Armstrong are amazingly easy to repair. The inlaid linoleums are much more difficult to work with, much easier to damage while installing, and harder to fix.

The following chapters will give you a good idea whether the savings gained by doing it yourself will outweigh the risks. If you are a confirmed do-it-yourselfer, much of the preceding discussion will be of little concern to you. Installing floor covering is not much different from most other do-it-yourself household projects. It is a matter of common sense, practice, and know-how. If you read the instructions carefully, practice, and use your common sense, you should have no problem.

### Relative Costs for Installing

**Example 1:** Assume an installation of 25 square yards of cushioned vinyl linoleum with poor sub-floor requiring plywood underlayment.

*Possible dealer charges:*

Install plywood (7 sheets @ $15) ...... $105.00
Install linoleum (25 yards @ $3.50) ..... 87.50
Charges for handling stove and
refrigerator ......................... 10.00
   Total dealer labor charges .......... $202.50
Note: door metal (see Chapter 13), adhesive, and other supplies included in above.

*Your do-it-yourself costs:*

| | | |
|---|---|---|
| Nails for plywood .................... | $ | 3.00 |
| Floor filler for plywood seams ......... | | 5.00 |
| Adhesive for linoleum ................ | | 15.00 |
| Disposable trowel .................... | | 2.00 |
| Roller rental ....................... | | 3.00 |
| Door metal (3 feet @ 50¢) ........... | | 1.50 |
| Miscellaneous ...................... | | 5.00 |
| Total do-it-yourself cost ............. | $ | 34.50 |
| Gross savings ..................... | $168.00 | |
| Less your time (figure a full day or more) ............................ | | |
| Net savings ....................... | | |

In the above example, if plywood cost $11 per sheet and your linoleum cost $9.00 per square yard, your materials cost would be:

| | | |
|---|---|---|
| Plywood (7 × 11) .................... | $ | 77.00 |
| Linoleum (25 × 9) ................... | | 225.00 |
| Total materials ..................... | $302.00 | |
| Total materials and dealer installation charges ......................... | $504.50 | |

Your gross savings ($168.00) equals 33 percent of the dealer's total charge.

**Example 2:** Assume 25 square yards foam-backed carpet to be cemented with no floor repair required.

*Possible dealer charges:*

| | |
|---|---|
| Install carpet (25 square yards @ $2.50) | $62.50 |
| Door metal (2 doors @ $2.00) ......... | 4.00 |
| Total dealer labor charges ......... | $66.50 |

*Your do-it-yourself costs:*

| | |
|---|---|
| Adhesive .......................... | $15.00 |
| Door metal (6 feet @ 50¢) ........... | 3.00 |
| Disposable trowel .................... | 2.00 |
| Miscellaneous ...................... | 5.00 |
| Total do-it-yourself cost ............. | $25.00 |
| Gross savings ..................... | $41.50 |
| Less your time (perhaps three or four hours) .............................. | |
| Net savings ....................... | |

If your foam-backed carpet cost $7.00 per square yard, your total dealer cost would be $241.50. Your gross savings ($41.50) equals 17 percent of the dealer's total charge.

**Example 3:** Assume an installation of 25 square yards carpet and pad with no floor repair required.

*Possible dealer charges:*

| | |
|---|---|
| Install carpet and pad (25 square yards @ $2.50) ................................ | $62.50 |
| Door metal (2 doors @ $2.00) ......... | 4.00 |
| Total Cost ......................... | $66.50 |

*Your do-it-yourself costs:*

| | | |
|---|---|---|
| Tackless stripping (64 feet @ 10¢) ..... | $ | 6.40 |
| Door metal (6 feet @ 50¢) ........... | | 3.00 |
| Kicker rental ........................ | | 5.00 |
| Miscellaneous (blades, staples, etc.) ..... | | 3.00 |
| Total do-it-yourself cost ............. | $17.40 | |
| Gross savings ..................... | $49.10 | |
| Less your time (perhaps one day) .... | | |
| Net savings | | |

If your jute-backed carpet cost $9.00 per square yard and your pad $2.00, total dealer cost for carpet and pad would be $275.00 and total job cost would be $341.50. Your gross savings equals 14 percent of dealer's total charge.

*Note:* Actual dealer or professional rates vary from one region of the country to another. The examples show, however, that less-expensive floor coverings and greater labor costs produce a higher percentage of savings for the do-it-yourselfer. Also, dealer charges are usually the same for more expensive floor coverings of the same type. The more expensive the floor covering, the less your percentage of savings, and probably the greater the risk factor for you.

# 6  Floor Preparation

**TO REPAIR OR NOT TO REPAIR?**

Sometimes a floor is in such poor condition that it is impossible to install a new floor over it without making improvements first. It is a question of whether you think a new floor will look all right if installed over an old floor without any advance preparation. This chapter will help you decide whether your present floor needs help, and if so, how to fix it.

Thin and shiny materials tend to show imperfections which may exist in the old floor underneath. Therefore, carpet with a thick pad under it is often the answer to covering a poor floor. A ½-inch-thick saxony with a ½-inch foam pad, for example, can smooth out an amazing assortment of hills and valleys.

Some of the thick cushioned linoleums tolerate a somewhat less perfect floor than the thinner ones, especially if they have a dull finish and do not need to be cemented all over. Cementing all over causes the linoleum to conform exactly to every imperfection underneath. Goods that do not require cementing may bridge minor imperfections. (Be sure the manufacturer guarantees that a loose-laid linoleum will not stretch or bubble up later.)

In any case, any linoleum or tile which is to be cemented all over should have an excellent sub-floor with all seams, and nail or knotholes filled. The floor must also be sound all over (not bubbling up or loose in a few places). Problems in a subfloor do not go away just because they have been covered. They are very likely to cause problems in the new floor later.

**APPROPRIATE SUBFLOORS FOR LINOLEUM AND TILE**

1. Old inlaid linoleum is appropriate provided it still is well cemented all over, with no edges or seams curling up and no bubbles or holes. If such conditions exist they must be repaired. You may be able to nail down a few loose spots and fill a few bad areas with a floor filler, then sand the entire floor to remove wax and ensure that the adhesive will adhere. But if the old floor is really bad you had better take it up and start over or cover it with underlayment board. Taking up an old floor is easier said than done for two reasons. One, it simply can be a "bear of a job." Two, many inlaid floors are made with asbestos in the back. When you take up an old inlaid floor, it is necessary to sand away portions which remain stuck to the floor. Sanding asbestor can produce dust highly dangerous to your health. Most installers today will not sand asbestos, leaving it up to the customer to

51

remove the floor or suggesting going over the old floor with underlayment. (More about underlayment shortly.)

2. Old vinyl asbestos and asphalt tile are appropriate, but be sure none of the tiles are loose. If they are and cannot be stuck back down securely, you had better take them up or put down underlayment board. As with old inlaid floors, minor repairs may be possible with a floor filler. Follow by sanding.

3. Old solid vinyl and rubber tile are appropriate, but all of the cautions in numbers 1 and 2 apply. In addition, you must be sure an adhesive is available that will adhere to both the old floor and the new.

4. Old rotogravure is sometimes appropriate, but keep the following in mind. Technically according to manufacturers' specifications, except for Armstrong's new Interflex floors mentioned earlier, you should not attempt to cover an old rotogravure floor without first removing the clear vinyl wear layer from the old floor. No matter what the experts tell you, this is a very difficult and time-consuming job, and it usually does not work. Almost invariably, when you pull away the top skin some of the back comes with it. The manufacturers tell you that this need not happen, that you should be able to pull the surface up and leave the back of the goods intact and ready to receive a new floor. You do it by cutting through the floor every 6 inches, then pulling the surface up in 6-inch strips. However, if the back starts to lift off the floor, you may have to take up the whole thing. Once you are into that, you are back to the problem of removing and sanding asbestos. If only a few small sections of the back come up you may be able to fill them and sand. No matter what anyone says, the whole process is difficult. Therefore you may need to cover the old floor with underlayment board.

A number of installers have told me that they have been able to install a new floor over a basically sound old rotogravure flooring without any advanced preparation. They claim that the new all-purpose latex adhesives work very well in this situation. While I do not recommend that you do anything contrary to what the linoleum manufacturers specify, you might want to consider this alternative. If you do, be sure that the adhesive manufacturer guarantees that the adhesive you use will do the job.

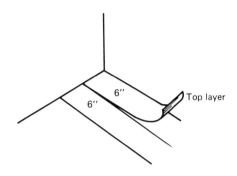

**Fig. 6-1** Rotogravure floor wear layer is pulled up more easily when cut through every 6 inches across width of room.

5. Hardwood floors are appropriate if you can tolerate ups and downs that may have developed through warping over the years. You also should keep in mind that while a hardwood floor may be perfectly smooth now, it can warp later. If you have a damp cellar underneath, a new nonporous floor installed over the old wood floor may prevent normal "breathing" in the old floor. Moisture can become trapped and cause an upheaval. Even a slight case of warping can create an unsightly condition later. The best way to avoid this problem is by putting down proper underlayment.

6. Plywood is appropriate as long as it is smooth, made with exterior glue, free of voids, and properly installed. (See How to Repair Your Floor—Linoleum and Tile).

7. Particle board is most emphatically NOT appropriate. With few exceptions, particle board is unacceptable as a subfloor for linoleum or tile.

8. The suitability of tempered Masonite and underlayments of similar composition has caused controversy among installers and dealers. (See How to Repair Your Floor—Linoleum and Tile.) Generally, if the linoleum manufacturer does not endorse a product as underlayment, you should not use it.

9. Concrete, above grade, is appropriate. Most linoleums and tiles can be installed over concrete. Just be sure the manufacturer says the particular one you want will work and that you use the right kind of adhesive. Make certain that if the concrete is new, it has cured properly and there is no moisture lingering in it.

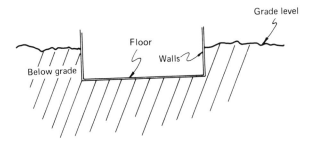

**Fig. 6-2** Level of floor is lower than the level of the ground outside, hence the term "below grade."

10. Concrete, below grade, might be appropriate. Below grade means the floor is below the level of the ground outside. Here you have to be very careful. You must be certain you have no moisture coming in from underneath, and that you will not have periodic flooding. Flooding is usually the result of improper drainage. Solve that problem before you attempt to install any kind of linoleum or tile. Moisture seeping up through the concrete may be the result of hydrostatic pressure. Since the floor is below the outside ground level, any water in the ground outside seeks its own level in your below-grade room as well as in all the area outside. Consequently, the water outside exerts a pressure on the water under the concrete floor, causing that water to force its way up through the concrete.

Many below-grade floors have no problem with moisture. But some do, and the problem may not show up until a floor has been installed and any moisture seeping up through the concrete is no longer able to evaporate into the room. You can test for moisture by taping a 1-foot-square piece of plastic to the floor on all four sides. Leave it overnight. If you do have hydrostatic pressure (or if the concrete is new and has not cured properly) you will find droplets of water on the underside of the plastic when you look at it next morning, unless conditions have been very dry outside for a long time.

Your moisture problem may not be caused by seepage. You may simply have a cold floor onto which moisture from warm air is condensing. This condition is revealed by the same test. Instead of being under the plastic, the moisture will be on top as well as on other areas of the floor. This means you may get condensation on the linoleum or tile after it has been installed, but as long as the

concrete is dry during installation the new floor will not be harmed. Carpet or a well-cushioned linoleum may solve the condensation problem by insulating the cold floor from the moist air. If you do have a moisture problem, do not attempt to install linoleum or tile until you have solved it.

## APPROPRIATE SUBFLOORS FOR CARPET

Most any floor, including particle board, properly cured concrete, and sometimes old carpet, can have almost any type of carpet installed over it. Just remember that the thinner the carpet and pad (or carpet alone, if no pad is to go under it), the more likely it is that imperfections will show through. The two areas in which you must exercise caution are covering below-grade concrete floors and covering old carpet installations.

As with linoleum and tile, you need to be careful with carpet in below-grade concrete situations if there is a moisture problem. However, the synthetic carpets are highly moisture resistant; as long as they are able to dry out after getting wet they should give you no lasting problem. They will not shrink, rot, or mildew. You have to be the judge as to what will work in your case. If your floor is constantly wet, you will have to correct this situation before you attempt to cover it. If you are only concerned that you might get a wet floor once in a while, here are some possible solutions:

1. If you expect only very infrequent flooding, consider installing an entirely synthetic (top and back) carpet and pad. You can rest assured that should the unlikely occur, your carpet will be all right once it has been taken up and dried out. So will the pad, but it might get damaged when you take it up for drying because most foam pads are fragile and become very heavy and hard to handle when loaded with water.

2. If you know that you have a periodic flooding problem, consider loose-laying an entirely synthetic carpet with no pad. You will give up the plushness of the pad, and you may have to put up with the carpet moving and bubbling a bit over the years, but when it gets wet you will be able to dry it out and put it back with little fear of damage.

3. If you have a slight case of hydrostatic pressure an entirely synthetic carpet, loose-laid, may work just fine because the moisture may evaporate

right through the carpet, causing no damage. However, a serious hydrostatic pressure problem can cause the carpet to become a sponge that never dries out.

4. Do not use foam-backed carpet if you have a moisture problem. Even though the foam is synthetic, it will act like a sponge, collecting water rather than drying out. Foam-backed carpet is inappropriate outdoors for the same reason. That is why I consider the term *indoor/outdoor* a misnomer for foam-backed carpets.

The only old carpet suitable as a subfloor is level-loop carpet that is cemented directly to the floor. If the new carpet is installed over an old level loop, this saves you the trouble of taking the old carpet up and provides a pad for the new one. You can install over the old carpet by trimming away the edges, putting down tackless stripping, and proceeding as with a standard tackless installation (see Chapter 9). Just be sure that the level-loop weave truly is a tightly woven level loop that will be an even pad under your new carpet.

Cut-pile and random-cut carpets should not be used as underlayment because they have a tendency to "grab" the bottom of the new carpet every time you walk on it and this pulls the carpet in the direction of the nap of the underlayment. This can cause all kinds of stretching and bubbling problems. Most of today's kitchen-type level loop, "indoor/outdoor" foam-backed carpets which have been cemented down all over will work just fine as a pad.

It is possible that the padding under the old carpet you are replacing can be used again. You may need to repair or replace a few areas where it has deteriorated, but it is often unnecessary to replace an entire floor of padding.

## HOW TO REPAIR YOUR FLOOR—CARPET

Usually you do not need to be quite as fussy about subfloor conditions when installing carpet as you do with linoleum. Therefore, you can probably repair the most glaring imperfections by using a floor-filling compound. There are many on the market; they usually come in one of two forms.

The first is the least expensive and simplest to use. It comes in powder form, is mixed with water, and acts and is applied much the same as

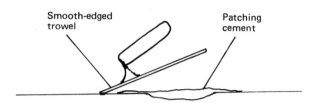

**Fig. 6-3** Floor irregularities can be filled with floor-filling compounds using a smooth-edged trowel to "feather out" edges of filler to the thinnest extent possible.

plaster of paris. Its disadvantages are that it sets up (hardens) very fast, so you can mix only a little at a time. Also, it tends to be brittle after it has set up, so it may crack over the years under your new floor if the subfloor has a tendency to flex.

The second type is a powder which is mixed with a solution of latex (often called *milk*). This type is more expensive, but the latex gives you more working time and is much less likely to crack with use.

Whatever type you use, be sure to read the label carefully before using it, as each manufacturer has specifications that must be followed if the product is to work correctly.

When applying the material use a smooth-edged trowel. Mix as much as you think you will need or can use before it sets up. Apply it to the depression you are filling and smooth it over with the trowel, allowing the edges of the filler to "feather out" to the thinnest possible extent. You cannot actually level your floor this way, but you can make the difference in level from one board or section of the floor to another seem to disappear. Sometimes several applications are required to get the desired results. If you try to apply too thick a coat at one time, the material may crack as it dries. Sandpapering the filler after it has set and dried will eliminate any imperfections left in the filler that you were not able to trowel away.

If you are repairing a linoleum or tile floor, be sure to cut away any loose material and nail down any edges which might curl up later, before you do any filling. Use underlayment nails (see Fig. 6-4), which do not "creep" back out later. An old wood floor, whether plywood, particle board, or hardwood, may need to be renailed in places to keep it from flexing and squeaking later on.

If the subfloor is in such poor condition that you feel even carpet cannot be installed over it without first putting down underlayment, see the next section. The only exception to what is stated there is that while you should not use particle board under linoleum, you can under carpet. If you install a carpet with pad, you normally do not have to fill and sand seams and nail holes in the new underlayment.

## HOW TO REPAIR YOUR FLOOR— LINOLEUM AND TILE

All of the instructions for carpet apply to preparing your floor for linoleum and tile. Regarding floor fillers, you need to be very fussy with the final results, or imperfections may show up after the new floor is installed. Also, major undulations in the floor can create problems in installing a brittle floor such as VA tile.

For linoleum and tile, it often is necessary to put down underlayment board. Plywood accepted by the American Plywood Association for this purpose is the only type of underlayment universally acceptable for use under linoleum or tile. It must be a good quality plywood which has been plugged and sanded, and which has been laminated with exterior glue. The linoleum manufacturers do not guarantee that their products will perform correctly if they are installed over any type of particle board unless it is a tempered hardboard that they have made and recommended for that purpose. For example, Armstrong makes a tempered underlayment board, and guarantees that you will have no problems with your linoleum as far as the subfloor is concerned if it is installed over their product. If you do use underlayment board supplied by the linoleum manufacturer, be sure you follow explicitly all the installation directions that accompany the board. Different boards may require different nailing procedures and spacings between boards.

Most particle boards, tempered or otherwise, are unacceptable because the linoleum manufacturers have no control over what goes into them. Particle boards can be very unstable, expanding and shrinking according to various weather and moisture conditions. They have been known to

Underlayment nail

**Fig. 6-4** The rings on the nail prevent the nail from coming back out. Cement-coated nails with the same property also are available.

shrink to such an extent that the linoleum has been pulled apart. While carpet can move with a moving subfloor, linoleum and tile, with few exceptions (such as Armstrong's do-it-yourself floors which can go over almost anything), cannot.

Another problem with particle board is that it can be quite difficult to fill and sand the seams after it has been nailed down. The board may crumble along the edges when sandpaper is applied, and attempting to set nails below the board surface with a hammer can cause the board to break.

Most floors can be repaired adequately with ¼-inch-thick plywood. If your existing floor is really bad you may need to use a floor filler prior to installing the plywood. Or you may need to use a thicker, more substantial plywood, ½ or even ⅝ of an inch thick.

When you install the plywood be sure to use proper underlayment nails. These are either cement coated or ringed with grooves so that once they have been nailed in they do not work back out. The board should be nailed every 6 to 8 inches along its width and length, and every 3 inches at the seams. If you use fewer nails you run the risk of having bubbles develop at a later date.

Be sure to check each sheet for voids. These are air pockets that occur in the plywood because the inner laminates have knotholes in them that have not been plugged by the manufacturer. The surface laminates will have been plugged, but there is no guarantee that the inner sheets have. Therefore, you should take a hammer and tap the sheet all over after you have nailed it down. If there is no void the plywood will feel firm as you strike it. If you suddenly feel a "punky" or soft spot, you probably have found a void. Strike harder, and the material will probably give way under the hammer. You also can cut the spot open with a knife. Cut

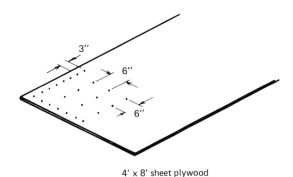

4' x 8' sheet plywood

**Fig. 6-5** Nail underlayment at 6-inch intervals all over and every 3 inches at the seams.

away the bad area (usually no more than a 3-inch area). Then, when you fill your seams and hammer impressions, you can also fill the void.

When installing an underlayment piece smaller than the standard 4-by-8-foot sheet of plywood, make careful measurements to be sure that the new piece will fit tightly against the one just nailed down. If you have a complicated wall section or doorway around which you must fit your underlayment, you may need to scribe a pattern on the plywood before cutting it. You can employ the same method described in Chapter 10 for pattern- or wall-scribing linoleum.

While you may not need to fill and sand the seams and nail holes in the underlayment for a carpet installation, you definitely should for linoleum. Even beautifully fitted plywood seams will show through a thin, cemented linoleum or tile. Nails should be well set into the plywood, and hammer impressions filled. Normally these are relatively minor imperfections and you will not need the latex-type filler. The simpler, water-based floor filler should work perfectly well. Finally, you should sand the floor lightly to be sure you have not left any little bumps and crevices that might show through later.

# 7 The Easier Carpet Installation

The easiest way to install a floor covering is to roll it out and walk away from it. You can do just that with an area rug. An area rug is simply a piece of floor covering—it can be linoleum as well as carpet—which covers an area of your floor but not all of it. When it is rolled out it will probably leave a border of the old floor uncovered. While it will not be wall to wall, it can be designed to cover most of your floor, if you wish. In fact, an area rug can, in theory, be made any size and almost any shape you want. There are limitations, however. First, the manufacturer's width limitations (discussed earlier) will apply in fitting a rug to your room. Second, some carpets, when not installed wall-to-wall, need to be bound. A tape or overlock stitch must be applied to the edge to prevent unravelling. Binding a square or rectangular rug should not be a problem for most dealers, but binding an irregular shape, say, a fireplace hearth cutout, may have to be done in your home right on the floor being covered. This added expense may well cancel out savings to be made by not choosing a wall to wall installation. And, if you are to do it yourself, you will soon discover that you might just as well install it wall to wall. If the rug has to be cut down, you may need to go through all of the trouble of a loose-lay installation plus the added aggravation of binding.

If you have a basically square room, and can tolerate a few inches of floor showing around the edges of the rug after it has been spread, the area rug may be the one for you. The dealer should be able to cut the rug to the size you wish and bind it, if necessary, and you should be able to just roll it out and be done with it.

## THE LOOSE LAY—FOAM BACK

The loose lay is the easiest type of wall-to-wall installation. It requires spreading out the carpet and trimming it in. No fastening is needed, except perhaps in doorways and at seams, and no stretching. Just spread it and trim it. Once you have become used to working with the tools and the carpet, you will undoubtedly agree that it really is that simple. This is especially true if you start with a foam-backed shag or sculptured shag, as discussed earlier.

One possible disadvantage, however, is that a loose-laid carpet can move to some extent. And it may well stretch in time due to the constant flexing of the back of the carpet caused by traffic. This can create bubbles. No dealer can guarantee that such problems will not occur. The way to avoid stretching and bubbling is to cement the carpet to the

**Fig. 7-1** Any hardware store sells a utility knife similar to the one shown above.

**Fig. 7-3** Cross section of "quarter round."

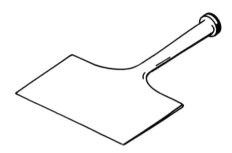

**Fig. 7-2** Because of curved corners installers use a "stair tool" in place of the screwdriver or putty knife suggested in text. (Carpet may be damaged by sharp corners.)

floor all over, not just around the edges. While cementing around the edges may prevent movement sideways, it will not prevent the carpet from stretching and then moving upward in the form of bubbles.

All of the techniques involved in the loose-lay installation apply to cementing your carpet, so let's proceed with the loose lay and then you can decide whether you want to cement it.

Start with a so-called "square room," which has only four walls and requires no seams. Once you have an understanding of the basics you can proceed to apply them to some more difficult areas. The tools you will need are a utility knife with new blades, a very dull screwdriver or other blunt instrument (such as a stiff putty knife or broad chisel), a good pair of scissors, and a hammer.

First, be sure that your floor is clean and free of anything that might stick up through the carpet after you are finished. If you are going to cement the carpet, have the floor as free of dust as possible. Next, decide what type of metal, if any, is to be used in the doorways, and install it now if this is called for (see Chapter 14).

Now spread out the carpet. You learned in the chapter on measuring that you should always add at least 3 inches to your room measurements as a

margin for error. Therefore, you now have a piece of carpet which, when spread out, will ride up the walls at least 1½ inches unless one or two of your walls line up with one or two of the edges of the carpet. If you can line up your carpet in such a manner then you will have eliminated approximately one-fourth or even half of the trimming necessary. The professionals always look for the easiest way out, and you might as well too. Another tip—if you are involved in new construction, you may want to leave your baseboards off until the carpet has been installed. Trimming will be much easier, and installing the baseboards after the carpet will allow you to cover a multitude of sins. Also, you can install the door frames so that they are raised slightly from the floor. Then the carpet can be trimmed a little long and tucked under the door frames.

With old construction it can help to remove the baseboards if they will come off and go back on easily. However, damage may result in trying to remove old baseboards, and you should not do this unless it is an extremely simple process. You'll soon discover that trimming the carpet is not that difficult, and it probably is not worth the trouble of fooling with the baseboards.

Your room may have a quarter-round molding running around the perimeter of the room at the bottom of the baseboards. Many older homes in New England have it. A quarter round is a quarter of a dowel. A one-half-inch quarter round, for instance, is a dowel 1 inch in diameter that has been cut lengthwise into four quarters. It is just about impossible to trim against quarter round molding. You should remove the quarter round and probably figure on throwing it away, since it may splinter. You might consider using some new quarter round to cover your mistakes after you have trimmed the carpet in against the baseboards.

After you have spread out your carpet, check to make sure the carpet is lying flat, that there are no wrinkles in it, and that any pattern or grain in the design of the carpet is running true to the room—not off on a disturbing angle which may be visually displeasing. There may be a few bubbles and the ends may seem to want to curl up if you have spread it properly. Curling is usually due to the fact that the carpet was rolled up for awhile. After a period of time it will settle down. Foam-backed carpets are designed to lie flat.

Now that your carpet is spread, you are going to "rough-cut" your carpet in. As you will soon discover, this is necessary in order to eliminate all stress points where the carpet is unable to lie on the floor the way it wishes it could. (Yes, it does sometimes seem to have a will of its own.) Also, you want to get rid of all excess material which would otherwise be in your way when making your final trim.

When you have spread the carpet out you will find that the edge of the carpet tends to drop into the doorway. This is a stress point. There is no wall for the edge to curl up against, and it wants to lie flat but can't. You will need to make a cut here to relieve the stress. Some doorways have a fancy trim or molding around them which protrudes into the room farther than the baseboard. You need to make a cut in the carpet here to eliminate stress so that the carpet can be "ironed-in" completely. (We'll get to ironing shortly.) You will also have to cut at each protrusion in the doorjamb.

Where the carpet is dropping into the doorway, fold back the carpet so that you have exposed the back and it is just touching the door frame at the fold. Note the point where there is no longer any wall or door trim to support the carpet. Draw a line on the back of the carpet from that point back to the edge of the carpet, on an angle of less than 90 degrees from the wall which is supporting the carpet, and away from the doorway. (The tip of your knife will scribe a mark in the foam back of the carpet.) When you cut through from the back along this line, the carpet will fall into the doorway and curl up against the door frame as it does along the wall.

Do not try to cut a perfect line which will cause the carpet to fall in place without trimming (except around the doorjamb or other sharp protrusions). This is very difficult to do, and you may end up with your carpet too short. You might as well figure on doing a little extra trimming and getting it right. You may have to finish your cut with

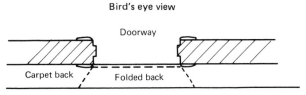

Bird's eye view

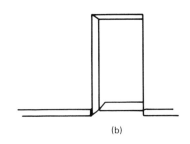

Fig. 7-4 Cut carpet with utility knife from the back at the angle shown.

scissors. Synthetic yarns can be very tenacious. A knife often will not cut through on the first or even second try. With a level-loop-weave carpet, hacking away at the cut with a knife may cause you to pull the yarn right out of the back, making it very unsightly. Finishing the cut with scissors will prevent all of these problems.

As a final step in the rough-cutting you should cut away all excess carpet. Sometimes having a lot of carpet riding up a wall makes it very difficult to iron-in the carpet and then to trim. It just gets in the way. However, you do not want to have *too little* carpet to trim either, as it can become very difficult to get the carpet to stay in place while you are trimming. At least one-half inch of carpet riding up the wall gives it the amount of rigidity you need while trimming. While you probably can tolerate as much as four to six inches of excess carpet in your way, I recommend that you trim off the excess, leaving about 1 or 2 inches for trimming if possible.

You are now ready to iron your carpet in. You are going to force a crease or fold into the carpet at the point where the floor meets the wall. Do this by first running your hand along the edge of the carpet, pressing firmly into the crease. The foam back will tend to stick to the wall and floor, holding the crease until you come back to it. Your hand will not produce a perfect enough crease, so you should go back over it with a dull (round-cornered)

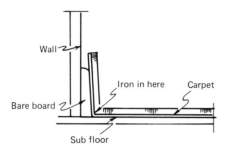

**Fig. 7-5** Force carpet to fold at juncture of floor and baseboard by ironing in with a stair tool or appropriate substitute.

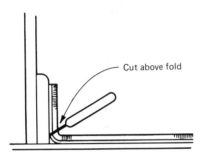

**Fig. 7-6** Cut ironed-in carpet above the fold.

screwdriver, putty knife or similar tool, forcing the carpet into that crease. The carpet should fold at a 90-degree angle where it rises up the wall from the floor.

Now take your utility knife. Start with a brand-new blade. Synthetic yarns are very difficult to cut with a dull blade. Apply the blade to the carpet slightly above the fold. If you cut into the fold itself your carpet will be short of the wall when you finish. This is because the foam behind the carpet has prevented you from getting that fold completely into the joint between the floor and the wall. Be reasonably bold with your knife. Make a firm cut for about a foot or two, then pull away the trimming and see how you have done. If you have cut too high above the fold, the carpet will be too long. If it is too long you can trim a little more off either with the knife (after ironing the carpet in again) or with a sturdy pair of shears. If the carpet is just slightly short, chances are the yarn will hide this fact. If you have made a bad cut, you can take a little of the trimming, cut off a piece, and fill the space. A shag makes this very easy. If you have made a really bad cut and you have not trimmed

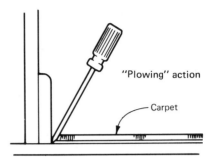

**Fig. 7-7** After trimming, tuck "fuzzies" between carpet and baseboard by running a screwdriver along the edge holding blade at angle to cause a "plowing" motion.

the opposite wall, you may be able to move the carpet over and start again, using up some of that margin for error excess you ordered.

By the time you have cut a few feet, you will have discovered the position your knife blade should be in and the rest of the room will go in quite easily. If you are installing different qualities of carpet in other rooms, you will find that each carpet cuts differently. You should always test the position of your knife a bit before getting carried away with the final trim.

When you have finished trimming you can tuck the yarn further down along the edges, if you wish. You probably will not feel this is necessary with a shag, but a level-loop weave may have some fuzzing where the loops have been cut in trimming. To eliminate fuzzing, you can take your dull screwdriver or other ironing tool and run it along the edge to create a plowing action that causes the blade of the screwdriver to push the yarn down between the edge of the carpet and the baseboard.

Once you have finished trimming and tucking, you may find it necessary to fasten the carpet down in the doorways to prevent anyone from tripping over the edges. The easiest way is to use some double-faced tape, about 1½ inches wide with adhesive on both sides. Pull the carpet back from the doorway. Cut off enough tape for the width of the doorway. Press it to the floor *just under the edge* of the carpet. Then carefully remove the paper backing from the tape. Let the carpet fall back into place and press down.

If you are installing metal trim in the doorways, it will be wise to use double-faced tape here, too. This will prevent the carpet from slipping out from under the metal later on.

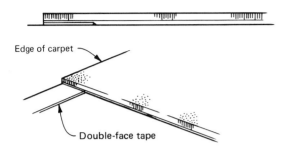

**Fig. 7-8** Place double-face tape just under the edge of carpet.

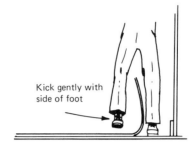

**Fig. 7-9** This technique can be used to move carpet short distances.

## THE LOOSE LAY—MORE DIFFICULT AREAS

Now you can tackle rooms with large cutouts in them, such as a chimney that protrudes into the room. (See Fig. 1-3.) Large cutouts make it more difficult to spread out the carpet in the first place and to rough-cut it in. Once you have overcome that difficulty, you are back to the basics of installing in a square room, with a few more edges to trim.

Assume you have a room that is 11½ feet wide and 13 feet long. The only problem is that on one of the walls there is a chimney sticking out into the room 2 feet, and it is 3 feet wide. How do you get a carpet that is 12 feet by 13 feet 3 inches spread out? First unroll the carpet as best you can in the largest area available. I often start by grasping the end of the carpet that is exposed on the outside of the roll and pulling hard right up to the ceiling. This pulls 7 or 8 feet free. Then you can unroll the rest of the carpet right in place so that it ends up in a pile in the middle of the floor. Now work one end of the carpet down to the nearest end of the room. Then pull the other end to the opposite end of the room, past the chimney. Now get the main area of the carpet spread out and as wrinkle free as possible, with the edge opposite the chimney riding up the wall the proper amount for ironing and trimming.

One way to move the carpet short distances is to stand at the edge of the room toward which you want the carpet to move. Pick up the edge of the carpet and place one of your feet on the bare floor and the other foot on the carpet. Pull the carpet up between your legs and place all your weight on the foot which is resting on the bare floor. Now you can gently kick or nudge the carpet in the direction

you want it to move with your free foot. Be careful, though. Foam-backed carpet has a weak back, and you could kick a hole in it. If the rubber back seems to stick to the floor, you can stand with both feet on the bare floor, grasp the edge of the carpet and get some air under it by flapping it much the same way you would a blanket on a bed. If you pull in the direction you want the carpet to move while getting some air under it, it will come right to you.

Next, make a fold in the carpet parallel to the wall the chimney is on, with the fold just touching the chimney. Now measure from the wall to the fold and compare that measurement with one from the fold to the edge of the carpet which you have folded back. The latter should be longer. This is to be sure you have folded back enough carpet so that it will fall into place correctly once you make a cut.

It is now time to rough-cut your carpet. Follow the square room instructions for rough-cutting in doorways. Then follow the same principles for rough-cutting around the chimney. Draw a line in the back of the carpet from each corner of the chimney to the edge of the carpet to which you are going to make your cuts. You can make sure you will be cutting in the right direction by finding the point on the edge of the carpet which is opposite the center of the three-foot chimney. Draw a line from each corner of the chimney to that point. Then make your cut from each corner to that point. This will make it possible for the carpet to fall past the chimney with carpet rising up the two-foot chimney walls as well as the three-foot wall. Of course, you can save the chimney cutout (perhaps to be used as a doormat) by not cutting to the center point as described above. Cut to a point closer to opposite the corners of the chimney. Just

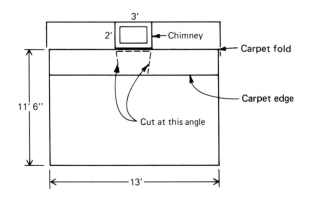

**Fig. 7-10** Be careful not to kick a hole through foam-back carpet. This view illustrates angles to use when rough-cutting around "cutouts."

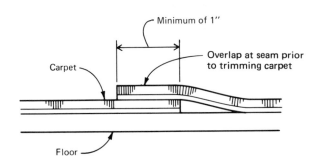

**Fig. 7-11** Allow no less than a 1-inch overlap at seams when spreading and rough-cutting carpet in.

be sure you do not go too far in the other direction or your carpet will be short on each 2-foot wall of the chimney. Now you can cut off the flap of carpet which the chimney has left you. Cut from the back leaving 1 or 2 inches to be ironed-in and trimmed.

Having accomplished the above you may now proceed to iron-in and trim the carpet as described in the square room section.

## THE LOOSE LAY—JUTE BACK

In this book, most references to jute-backed carpet include jute-backed carpets and all other carpets which do not have foam backs. They may have second backs of jute or other synthetic substitutes such as Loctuft or ActionBac.

All of the instructions regarding foam-back loose-lay installation apply to jute-backed carpet. Jute-backed carpets, however, may have slight disadvantages. They normally do not hold their ironed-in position as well as do foam backs, and they tend to be more stiff and difficult to work with. These are relatively minor problems that can be overcome. You may, for instance, have to hold the ironed-in crease with one hand while you cut with the other. When doing so be sure not to let one hand get behind the blade. A sudden release of the knife could cause a nasty cut.

## SEAMS

Assume that you have read the directions on measuring, determined that your carpet must be

installed in more than one piece, and decided where the seam is to be located.

When spreading out your carpet, follow all the directions regarding the rough-cut just discussed in the section called Loose Lay—More Difficult Areas. Where you are joining two pieces of carpet with a seam, let the carpet overlap on the edges by at least 1 or 2 inches.

If you are loose-laying your carpet you should make your final cut for the seam and fit your seam together before you do the final trim along the wall. The seam is usually the area most vulnerable to mistakes. By not trimming at the walls first, you leave yourself room to shift the carpet over a bit at the seam and begin again.

Once you have your carpet spread out and rough-cut, your first step in preparing the seam is to trim the edges which are to be joined. Never use the carpet edge cut by the factory. No matter how good that edge may look, it is not good enough. Of course, there are exceptions to all rules—with a short shag or sculptured shag you may feel the edges of your carpet go together beautifully and require no preparation. But don't count on it. With any type of carpet you must be very certain that the edges are as close to perfect as you can get them.

With some level-loop carpets, it is possible to trim the edges by using nothing more than a good pair of scissors. All level-loop carpets have a pattern or direction in the yarn which runs along the length of the roll. This is because the strands of yarn have been inserted in a continuous row from one end of the roll to the other. Sometimes these rows are very straight. Other times they are crooked. If they are straight, you can make a

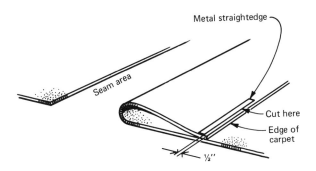

**Fig. 7-12** Use straightedge as a guide to cut from back of carpet.

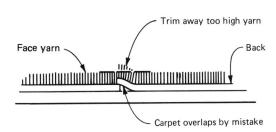

**Fig. 7-13** Overlapping edges of finished seams cause unsightly condition. This can be corrected by trimming too-high yarn to surrounding level with scissors.

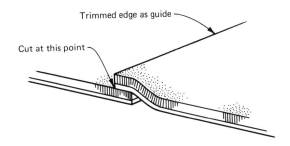

**Fig. 7-14** Using newly trimmed edge as a guide, trim away other edge.

cutting guideline by taking hold of an end of yarn that is exposed at the edge you wish to trim, and pulling it. The yarn will pull out along the entire length of the edge, leaving the back exposed where the yarn came out. When you trim away this back with your shears, cutting as close to the next row without cutting into it as you can, you may produce an excellent edge for seaming. You may even be able to do this with both edges. If they go together satisfactorily, leaving no gaps or overlaps when you butt the edges along the entire seam, you'll be ready to make your seam.

However, most carpets, including many level loops, cannot be trimmed in this manner. They require that you cut the edge away with a sharp knife, cutting from the back in the following manner.

Fold the carpet back 2 or 3 feet, exposing the back so that it lies flat. Using a straightedge of some sort (a carpenter's square, yardstick, or any item you may have that has a straight edge on it, preferably metal) as a guide for your knife, cut away about ½ of an inch from the edge.

By cutting from the back you will cut away practically none of the face yarn. This will ensure that it remains at exactly the length it was intended to be. If you cut from the front, your knife blade will catch some of the yarn and shave it away, leaving many of the strands much shorter than they should be. If you try to put two shaved edges together, you will find that an unsightly valley has been created along the seam.

If you are making a short seam, you may be able to create suitable edges by cutting with a straightedge as described. Put the two together; if you really have cut two straight edges, they should

match nicely. When you join the seam, have the back of each edge touch the other. Do not let them overlap. If they overlap, one edge will appear higher than the other, creating an unsightly condition. However, if you find that you have let the edges overlap slightly, you may be able to correct the unevenness by trimming down the yarn that's too high to the level of the surrounding yarn. If, on the other hand, they do not butt perfectly and there is a gap, you probably can stuff in a little yarn with some glue (such as Elmer's) to make things look much better. These remedies should work with deep-pile carpets such as shags and plushes.

If you are making a long seam, you probably will not be able to cut a perfectly straight edge along its entire length. When dealing with fabrics you have to resign yourself to the fact that the material is not as stiff as, say, a board, and it will shift a bit now and then while you are working with it. Therefore, perfectly straight cuts are rare. You may have to cut your second edge using your first as a guide. Let the edges overlap, with the newly

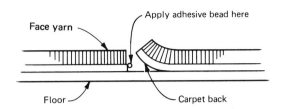

**Fig. 7-17** Bead of adhesive at the base of the yarn is essential to prevent yarn from pulling out later. This is especially important with level-loop carpet.

**Fig. 7-15** Specially designed trimming tools help trim second edge of carpet using first edge as a guide.

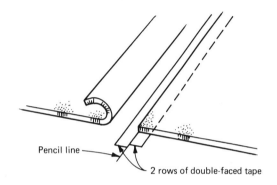

**Fig. 7-16** Double-face tape under both edges will help prevent the seam from moving later on.

trimmed edge on top. Using this edge as a guide, cut through the carpet underneath with a utility knife that has a brand-new blade. You will be cutting from the top, therefore shaving away some of the face yarn. Take care to minimize the shaving away. Specially designed knives are available for this purpose. These trimming tools help the blade find a path between the strands of yarn. They also help you to follow the guiding edge. If you are dealing with a short shag, saxony, or similar style, your utility knife will probably do the job. Any slight deviation from a perfect match probably will not show.

Once you have trimmed away the second edge, remove the trimmings from under the carpet and butt the two new edges together. You are now ready to make the seam.

If this is to be a loose-lay installation, your next step is to fold both edges back again and install two rows of double-faced tape on the floor directly under each seam edge. Fold back one edge. Using the other edge as a guide, draw a line on the

subfloor to indicate the seam. Fold this edge back and apply the tape. One-and-½-inch-wide tape will suffice, but 2-inch-wide tape is better. This gives a total of 4 inches of tape, 2 inches on either side of the seam. Now remove the protective coating from the double-faced tape under one edge only and let the corresponding piece of carpet fall back in place. Press this edge onto the tape.

To ensure that the yarn will not pull out, you must run a "bead" of adhesive along the edge of the carpet you have just dropped into place. The bead should be at the base of the face yarn at the point where the yarn enters the back. Special adhesives are available for this purpose, but you can use Elmer's or any white glue. While these glues are a bit stiff once they dry, they will do, and chances are you already have some in your house.

Once you have run the bead of adhesive along this edge you can replace the second edge after removing the protective coating. Be sure to keep the face yarns out of the bead of adhesive. The bead of adhesive will adhere to the second edge also, creating a contact between the two. Gluing helps ensure that no yarn will come out along the edges of the seam and that the edges will stay together. White glues tend to dry clear so that initial unsightliness should disappear. If you get too much white glue on the carpet, you can remove it with water if you catch it before it dries. Some latex adhesives developed for carpet seams require special solvents for cleaning. If you decide to use one of the latex adhesives, be sure you have some solvent at hand for emergency use, and follow directions given by the adhesive manufacturer.

Now that you have made the seam, you can proceed to install your carpet as described in the earlier sections of this chapter.

# 8 Cementing Your Carpet

Cementing your carpet is simply one more step beyond the loose-lay installation. It ensures that your carpet will not move and bubble up over its years of use. You can cement both foam-backed and jute-backed carpets (no pad underneath). All of these instructions apply to both types of fabrics.

Cementing takes place after the rough-cut and before the final trim (including the seam). The carpet might shift a bit while you are cementing. If you make your final trim first you have left no margin for slight movement while cementing.

If there is no seam, fold back your carpet until you have exposed approximately one-half of the floor. If you are working alone, a good technique for folding a large section back is to do it in these three phases. First, grab one corner and fold it back to the center of the room. Then grab the opposite corner and do the same. This will leave two triangles of floor exposed along the two end walls of the area to be cemented. You'll have a triangle of carpet waiting to be folded back. Now grab the corner at the peak of the triangle created by the first two folds, and fold it back across the room. The carpet will be much less bulky to handle this way, and less likely to get out of control when you replace it after cementing.

Now apply the adhesive. (See Adhesives in this chapter.) Then put the carpet back in place. With your hands, you should press the carpet down all

over so that you are sure it has made contact with the cement all over. At this point you can make a final trim in the area where the carpet has been cemented. Or you can wait until the entire area is cemented. Now fold back the other half, exposing a little of the already cemented area, and apply your adhesive, making sure you have covered all of the floor over to where the first application of adhesive was made. Then place this section back down, press the carpet into the adhesive, and trim.

If you are making a seam, follow all of the instructions given thus far, but cement only to within a foot or so of the seam. After the main sections have been cemented and are firmly in place is the time to make your final trim along the edges of the seams. Once the final trim is done and you are ready to put the edges together permanently, fold them back and apply your adhesive. Then allow one edge to drop in place. Apply the bead of white glue or special seam adhesive, and put the second edge in place. (See Seams in Chapter 7.)

You may find when cementing a seam after trimming that the edges have a tendency to overlap. (When you put the edges together in the loose-lay situation, your main pieces tend to back up a bit so that any overlap problem is alleviated.) The overlapping of cemented pieces will not retreat by itself. This is all right as long as the overlap

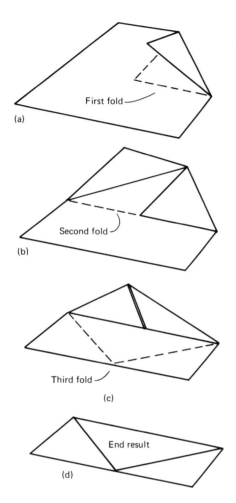

**Fig. 8-1** When working alone, fold carpet back in 3 stages. First fold (a) exposes ⅓ of floor to be cemented. Second fold (b) exposes another third. Final fold (c) exposes entire section (d) desired.

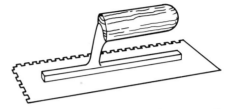

**Fig. 8-2a** Notched trowel used for spreading adhesive.

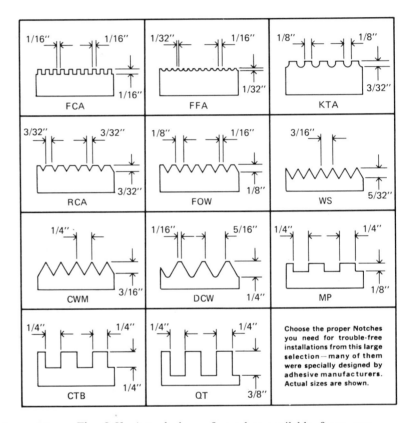

**Fig. 8-2b** Actual sizes of notches available from one manufacturer. (Courtesy the Gundlach Co.)

is slight. When putting your carpet together with the edges butting you will be creating a "compression" seam. Edges that overlap slightly can be compressed down into the adhesive to butt together tightly. This helps ensure that there will be no parting at the seams later. You will find that the carpet will press down into the adhesive and stay there once the adhesive has begun to set up.

## ADHESIVES

I recommend an all-purpose latex adhesive. Most of them are very easy to work with. They are water soluble while still wet so that initial clean up is easy.

Yet once set up they are basically waterproof so that the installation is truly permanent. Latex adhesives usually have an excellent "open time." This means that once you have applied the adhesive to the floor, you have 30 minutes or so to get your carpet trimmed in before the adhesive sets up. This gives you a little time to shift the carpet if you happen to make a mistake.

Be sure to read the label on the can of adhesive carefully and follow the manufacturer's instructions regarding the type of trowel to use and

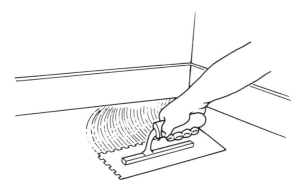

**Fig. 8-3** Draw trowel back and forth like a snow plow to spread adhesive.

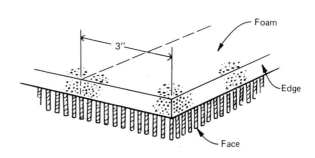

**Fig. 8-4** Trimming away foam back along the edges can eliminate unsightly bulkiness when folding edges under. Score along dotted line, then peel.

any special application instruction. Also be sure your floor is free of dust.

Adhesive is applied using a notched trowel. The edge of a notched trowel has teeth in it. The teeth can be of varying sizes. Different adhesives require trowels with different size teeth. When you pull the trowel over the floor with the adhesive in front of it, the size of the teeth determines how much adhesive stays on the floor.

When applying the adhesive, pour onto the floor only as much as you feel you can work with comfortably. Start in one corner of the room. Dip the edge of the trowel in the adhesive you have poured on the floor and then dab the adhesive in along the edges of the room, going as close to the wall as you can without getting the cement on the baseboards. Once you have applied the adhesive along the edges you can use a snow plow motion to work the adhesive back and forth until you have covered the floor. Be sure to work your way back toward the carpet so that you won't get stuck in a corner.

## STAIRS

When covering stairs with carpet you must be certain that the carpet is fastened securely. Otherwise, you can have a very unsafe condition. Do not attempt to put carpet on stairs with just a few tacks holding things in place. It will not work. If you are planning to put foam-backed or jute-backed carpet (with no pad) on stairs, you should cement it.

For this purpose you will need a trowel and adhesive, knife, "kicker" (see Fig. 9-10), staple gun, hammer, carpet tacks, and blunt screwdriver or stiff putty knife.

Your first step is to cut the carpet up exactly as you want it to go on the stairs—as a centered runner, wall to wall, or wall to banister. Presumably you figured this out when measuring for it in the first place. Or, if the dealer measured for you, he/she can draw a diagram showing how the cutting was figured.

If you have a reasonably "square" set of stairs, you'll probably be able to get more than one step out of a piece of carpet and won't have to cut each step separately. For the purposes of this discussion, assume that you are installing a runner on a straight set of stairs. Assume you want the runner to be 2 feet 3 inches wide and centered on the stairs. Your stairs require 18 to 20 feet of runner. If you have purchased a runner ready-made in the dimensions required, then you just have to cement it to the stairs. That will be explained shortly. If you have purchased some broadloom which you have to cut up into the desired sizes, consider the following suggestions.

First, the edges of level-loop-weave carpet must always be protected or they may unravel. Therefore, you should consider having them bound before you install the carpet. Your dealer may be able to do this for you. An alternative is to fold the edges under while installing the carpet. If you are going to fold the edges under, you'll need

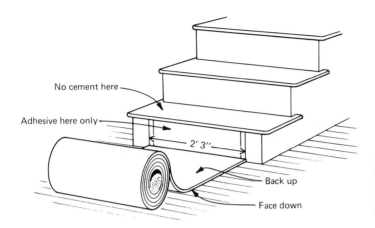

No cement here

Adhesive here only

2' 3"

Back up

Face down

**Fig. 8-5** Placing carpet as shown, with face down and bottom edge against bottom riser, protects floor underneath from spilled adhesive. At step 4 apply adhesive only on the bottom riser as indicated.

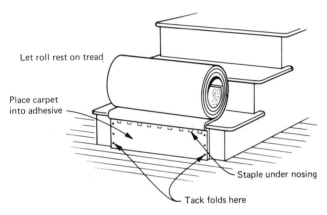

Let roll rest on tread

Place carpet into adhesive

Staple under nosing

Tack folds here

**Fig. 8-6** After step 6 your roll rests on first tread. Carpet is cemented on first riser and stapled under nosing. Folds, if needed, are tacked where shown.

to cut your runner extra wide (about 1½ inches extra on each edge), so that when folded under on the edges, the exposed width will be your desired width.

Folding under foam-backed carpet can create a bulky fold that looks unattractive. To avoid this you can trim away some of the rubber back. Turn the carpet on its back and score a line through the rubber layer only, about 3 inches in from and parallel to each edge. Be sure you do not cut into the fabric itself. Now peel the 3-inch strip of rubber off along the edges. It will come off to the line you have scored. This may be a bit painstaking, but the end result will be worth it.

Now you are ready to begin cementing. The following technique minimizes the risk of getting

cement anywhere but where it is supposed to go, and the carpet will go on quite easily.

First, mark on your stair treads with pencil or chalk, exactly where you want the edges of your runner to be. These marks will be 2 feet 3 inches apart if you want your runner to be 2 feet 3 inches wide.

Second, roll up the runner from top to bottom with the back facing out. The first end (the end to be fastened at the bottom of the stairs) should be exposed.

Third, place this end at the foot of the stairs against the bottom of the riser, exactly in position. The back should be up and the face of the carpet against the floor.

Fourth, apply some adhesive to the bottom riser only. Apply it only to within an inch or so of the edge of the runner. You can use the notched end of your trowel. Dip it into the pail of adhesive, removing small amounts each time.

Fifth, place the first eight inches or so of carpet exactly in place over the adhesive, folding the edges under (if called for) as you go along. To get the rest of the roll out of the way, let it rest on the first tread. That is why you did not put any adhesive there. Place some tacks on the folded edges to make them stay in place.

Sixth, with your staple gun push the carpet in under the first nosing. Apply one staple every 3 inches or so. Now that you have the folds tacked on this first riser and the staples in under the first nosing, you can proceed up the stairs.

Seventh, drop the remainder of the roll back onto the floor, being careful not to pull out the

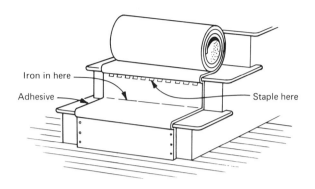

**Fig. 8-7** After applying adhesive to next tread and riser, spread runner as shown, ironing in where tread meets riser and stapling under next nosing.

staples. Apply adhesive to the first tread and second riser (not to the third tread).

Eighth, unroll the carpet a bit more until you have enough to place it on the first tread and second riser with the balance of the roll resting on the second (uncemented) tread. You can move the carpet gently, if necessary, with your kicker. (See Fig. 9-8.) With a blunt screwdriver, iron the carpet into the fold where the first tread meets the second riser. Then fit the carpet onto the second riser, folding the edges (if needed) as you go along. Staple under the second nosing and you are ready to proceed to the next tread and riser, and so on until you have used up your runner.

If you have to install the carpet in more than one piece, follow the same directions starting from the first again.

If you are installing carpet wall to wall on stairs, you can follow all of the eight steps except that you will not be folding the edges under. Instead, cut your carpet into a runner that will fit exactly wall to wall, and proceed as above. It is often difficult to work with a rolled up piece of carpet in a wall-to-wall installation, as the roll can become wedged in the stairway. If this happens, unroll the runner and let it extend on up the stairs lying flat. Do not push it in to conform to the steps and risers. If you do, it may get stuck in this position. As you move along up the stairs, you will need some slack to be able to push the carpet into each tread and riser as you come to it. If all of your steps are not exactly the same width, or you have winders, you will have to do some trimming-in as you go along. Cut the carpet a bit wider than

needed and proceed as described for a straight installation. When you need to trim, simply iron in and trim exactly as you would a room.

For a wall-to-banister installation, you will probably want to fold under the edge at the banister. Otherwise, all the eight steps apply.

## Upholstering

Upholstering is the process of wrapping the ends of the treads much as you would wrap a package. No two sets of stairs are the same, so upholstering requires a certain amount of imagination as you go along to be sure the end product looks the way you want it to.

First, cut your carpet so that the runner is wide enough to cover the end of the tread to the point you want it to go, with a little extra as a margin for error.

Second, cement the runner as has been described, but apply your adhesive only to the point where the carpet can be pressed comfortably into place as you work your way up the stairs, leaving dry those areas beyond the banister where you will have to fit the carpet for the upholstered effect. (See Fig. 8-8.) As you proceed up the stairs, make "relief" cuts at each point where the carpet rests against the rungs of the banister, allowing the carpet to drop through and "relax" while waiting for you to come back to it. Save the upholstering until you have all the main sections of carpet installed.

Third, start upholstering at the bottom step (see Fig. 8-10). Begin with the first riser. Find the point on the back of the carpet where the riser and nosing meet. Cut the carpet from that point out to the edge, on an angle heading toward the floor. You will be left with a flap that can be folded under on the riser so that the edge of the fold exactly conforms with the end of the riser. You will have too much material to fold, however. Cut off the flap so that it is only about 1½ inches wide. Then peel away the rubber back if you wish, fold under, and tack.

Fourth, find how much carpet you need for the carpet to fold over the top of the tread and under the nosing to the point you desire. Cut off the waste. Now wrap the corners of the treads as you would a package, getting the raw edges of carpet folded in out of sight. You may have to cut

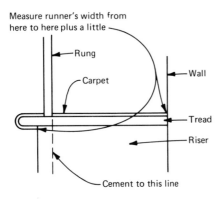

Fig. 8-8 Measure from wall through rungs and around end of tread for the width of runner. Add a little for good measure. Apply adhesive only to areas which can be comfortably worked prior to upholstering.

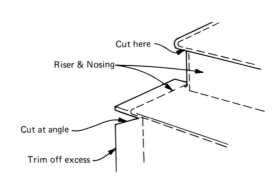

**Fig. 8-10**

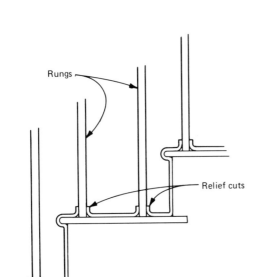

Fig. 8-9 End view showing edges of carpet falling through rungs of banister waiting for upholstering.

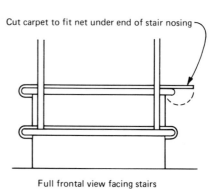

Full frontal view facing stairs

Fig. 8-11 Prior to wrapping, trim carpet to fit exactly under end of nosing.

away some excess material to eliminate bulkiness. Once you have it folded so that you like its appearance, you can tack it in place. Work both corners this way. You may find that in cutting the next riser from the first tread you do not have enough carpet to finish the back corner of the first tread. In this case you will need to use some scraps and fill out any bare spots as best you can. With short shags, saxonies, and other deep-pile carpets this is not usually difficult.

# 9 Tackless Installation

Before attempting a "tackless" installation you should read the preceding three chapters. These will give you an idea how carpet is handled. Further, many references will be made in this chapter that will make sense only if you have read Chapters 6, 7, and 8. Tackless installation is not appropriate with foam-backed carpet. Foam backs simply will not stand up to the stresses and strains of tackless installation. They are also unsuitable because tackless installation requires that a pad be installed under jute-backed carpet.

What is a tackless installation? In the early days of wall-to-wall carpet, padding was placed to within about 2 inches of the walls and was fastened in place. Then the carpet was spread over it, with an extra 2 inches riding up each of the walls. This extra material was folded under and tacked in place. The tacks were placed about every 1½ inches. This meant that there were little indentations in the carpet every 1½ inches. This technique took an awfully long time.

Tackless stripping (tackless) is a piece of plywood about $^9/_{32}$ of an inch thick, 1 inch wide, and 4 feet long. It has hundreds of little tacks protruding from its upper surface at an angle. It also has nails partly inserted down into it at about 5-inch intervals along its length so that it can be nailed to the floor. Tackless stripping with nails is called *prenailed* tackless. This is the type you will

need for most tackless installations. Tackless stripping can be used over both wood and concrete floors, but the nails used for wood are different from those used for concrete. Be sure you specify which you need.

In addition to tackless stripping, you will need a hammer, carpet tacks (or substitute for fastening tackless in places where the prenailing does not fit), staple gun and staples (⅜- to ½-inch), cutter for cutting the tackless stripping (a large pair of tin snips works very well), broad, dull chisel or similar tool (like an installer's stair tool), kicker, utility knife, and good scissors or shears.

The first step is to install the tackless and metal trim in doorways, as required. (See Chapter 13.) First, take several lengths of tackless (very carefully—it can cause punctures in your hands) and place the 4-foot lengths around the room at 4-foot intervals. This eliminates the need to run back and forth to your supply of tackless. Now start in a corner of the room and place one of the strips along the first 4 feet of the wall. Place it with the little tacks (called *pins*) up and with the angle of the pins pointing *toward the baseboard*. The tackless should be about ¼ to ⅜ of an inch from the baseboard along its length so that when the carpet is installed it can be tucked into the space between the tackless and the baseboard. Now hammer this first piece of tackless in place. If the wall is a bit

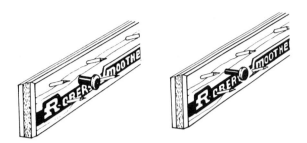

**Fig. 9-1** Tackless stripping. Two types are shown—one with heavier "drive pins" available for nailing into concrete. (Courtesy Roberts Consolidated Industries)

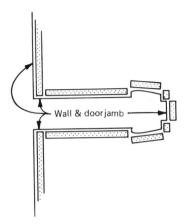

**Fig. 9-3** Pieces of tackless are cut to fit every nook and cranny.

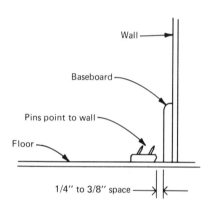

**Fig. 9-2** Tackless is fastened down about ¼ to ⅜ of an inch out from the baseboard with "pins" pointing toward baseboard.

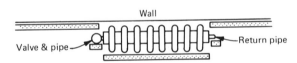

**Fig. 9-4** This view shows tackless installed in front of radiators and pipes with pins facing wall behind radiator.

curvy, you will find that the tackless can bend a bit to accommodate slight imperfections in the line of the wall.

As you go along fastening down your tackless, you will find that the 4-foot lengths do not always fit. Using your tin snips, cut off what you need and nail it in place. Be sure to have at least two nails in small pieces of tackless so that the pieces will not swivel later, and be sure there are nails at least every 5 inches. Fit the tackless to conform to every indentation and protrusion around the room. Tackless can be cut into pieces as little as an inch long for nailing around doorjambs, etc. If you have a radiator or baseboard heating, nail a strip or strips across the front of the appliance from one end to the other and as close to the appliance as you can get it. The carpet will have to drop in loose beyond the tackless under the radiator or heating unit, but it will be held in place immediately in

front. Also place a small piece of tackless in front of any pipes coming up through the floor, and always along any section of the baseboard you can reach. Forced-hot-air ducts or other holes in the floor which will be exposed after the carpet has been installed should have tackless nailed in place on all four sides. Remove the protective grille and nail the tackless as close to the hole as is possible without obstructing grille replacement. The pins should face into the hole on all four sides.

When you have finished you will have tackless around the entire perimeter of the room, about ¼ to ⅜ of an inch from the baseboards. All of the pins should be pointing toward their respective walls so that the pins on opposite walls are leaning away from each other.

Now place your padding. Most pads today come either 4½, 6, or 12 feet wide. Place the pad in

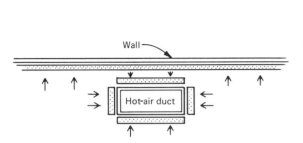

Fig. 9-5 Tackless placed close to edge of duct in floor. Arrows show direction of pins facing into the hole even along back edge while pins in tackless along the wall face the wall.

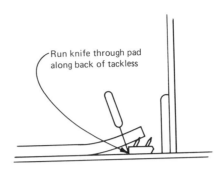

Fig. 9-7 Use the back edge of the tackless as guide for knife to trim away the pad where it overlaps the tackless.

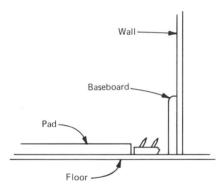

Fig. 9-6 Pad is installed *up to* the tackless, not on it.

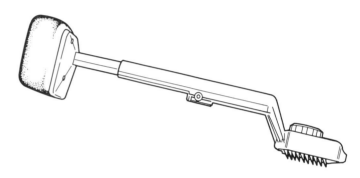

Fig. 9-8 Kicker has pins pointing down in front to grab carpet. Padded end absorbs shock from striking with the knee. (Courtesy Crain Cutter Co., Inc.)

the most efficient manner, with as little waste and as few seams as possible. Also try to keep pad seams away from where the carpet seams will be.

Install your pad up to the tackless, *not on it.* The pins are meant to hold the carpet, not the pad. Fasten the pad to a wood floor with your staple gun, placing staples about every 6 inches around the perimeter of the room and about every 3 inches along the seams. (A hammer-type stapler is best.) Cut the pad with a sharp knife or shears. You can use the inside edge of the tackless as a guide, and run the knife along bearing down to the floor.

Remember that the pad is not intended to be walked on except when covered by carpet. All you are doing with your pad is creating an additional layer of sponge or hair and jute to give the carpet added plushness and wear. Therefore, do not be overly concerned if you cut the pad wrong or if it gets ripped while you are installing it. Just put it down anyway and put a few extra staples in where

such cuts and tears occur. You can also use some 2-inch-wide duct adhesive tape to make sure seams stay secure. This is not essential. Many installers do not use tape, and extra staples along the seams may suffice.

The next step is to spread your carpet and rough-cut it in, getting rid of waste pieces as described in the earlier chapters. You now are ready to "kick" your carpet in.

Kicking-in carpet is a technique that accomplishes two things. First, it gets the carpet fastened to the tackless. Second and most important, it is a means of prestretching the carpet so that it will not bubble up later. Therefore it is necessary to follow a definite pattern as you kick your carpet in around the room. (You will need to rent or buy a kicker.)

At this point, however, we must digress a little to explain what a kicker is (see Fig. 9-8). A kicker is composed of a head, shaft, and padded tailpiece.

**Fig. 9-9** This shows position for "kicking" carpet. One hand grasps kicker, with corresponding knee behind pad on end of kicker. Weight is distributed evenly on hands and knees.

The illustration shows the head with many sharp pins protruding from its bottom at an angle pointing toward the front of the kicker. With most kickers, the depth of these pins is adjustable. Twisting a knob on the top of the head causes the pins to move up or down depending on the depth of the pile of the carpet. The pins are intended to penetrate the carpet pile to the back of the carpet. The padded end of the kicker is struck with the part of your leg immediately above the knee—not with the knee proper. When you strike the kicker you force it forward. If the pins are imbedded in the carpet, it moves at the same time. The technique is as follows.

Get on your hands and knees. If you are right-handed, grasp the kicker by the shaft with your right hand. The pins should be imbedded in the carpet with the bottom of the padded end resting on the carpet. Place your right knee on the carpet immediately behind the padded end. Put your left knee approximately 6 inches (whatever gives you a sense of balance) to the left, and even with the right knee. Place your left hand on the carpet to the left. You should now be resting on all fours in a comfortable balanced position. Now transfer all your weight to your two hands and your left knee. Lift your right knee a bit off the carpet and pull it back a comfortable distance. Now strike the kicker on the pad with your right knee. The force of that strike will cause the kicker and the carpet underneath to move. The greater the force, the more it will move. You can do it very gently or with great gusto depending on what is required. An additional technique which you will develop is to lift your entire weight off your left knee as your right knee strikes the kicker. Then the kicker will only have to move the weight of the carpet, not your weight also. *Be very careful if working with foam-backed carpet.* There is very little strength in the foam back. You should only use the kicker very gently for making minor adjustments. Many carpet professionals have learned this the hard way by taking a section of carpet exactly the size of the kicker's head out of a foam-backed carpet. The same can be true of some less expensive jute-backed carpets.

Now back to the tackless installation. The first step in getting the carpet fastened down is to hook it onto the tackless. Tools needed are the kicker, a broad, dull chisel (or other instrument for tucking) and a sharp (new blade) utility knife.

Start along a 2- or 3-foot section of wall in one corner of the room. Make sure you have all excess waste cut away. Have no more than 3 or 4 inches of carpet riding up the wall. In corners, you may find that even this excess causes bulkiness that makes kicking the carpet in difficult. Cut away the excess at this point as close to a net trim as you can.

Now place the kicker on the carpet with the front of the head just in front of the tackless (you can feel the tackless through the carpet with your fingers). Strike the kicker with a medium blow. This will cause the carpet to move across the pins of the tackless which are pointing toward the wall. At this point keep the kicker in position; do not lift it away. The carpet will have a tendency to retreat to its original position after the initial blow. As it does, with the front of the kicker still resting over the tackless, the carpet will be trapped by the pins and hook onto the tackless.

Next, keeping your right hand on the kicker, take the dull, broad chisel (tucker) and tuck the carpet into the space left between the tackless and the baseboard. The tucker will force the back of the carpet to fold at the bottom of the baseboard.

Now switch your weight to the tucker. Hold the carpet on the tackless and fold it into the space between the tackless and baseboard with the tucker. Then lift your kicker with your right hand and move it along the wall about 4 to 6 inches. Now repeat the kicking procedure. Once you have kicked the carpet on at this second position, move your tucker along to force the carpet in at this new point. The first position will usually remain hooked after you remove the tucker. Again, keeping your weight on the tucker, move along and repeat the operation. Keep this up until you have hooked the carpet on for 2 or 3 feet. The first

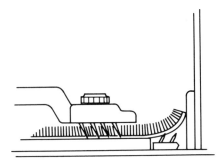

**Fig. 9-10** First place head of kicker immediately in front of tackless.

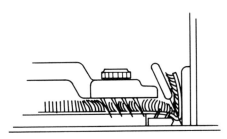

**Fig. 9-11** Tuck carpet to fold in gap between tackless and wall. Kicker holds carpet on pins while you tuck with broad chisel or other suitable tool.

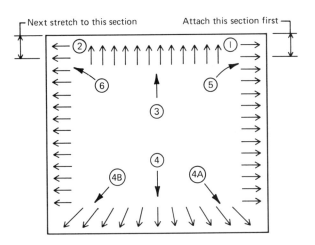

**Fig. 9-12** Kicking and stretching patterns described in text.

few feet you have hooked on should stay on. This operation involves a bit of technique. Don't be discouraged if it doesn't work at first. All of a sudden it will, and there will be no explanation why. Just persist.

Now it is time to make your first "stretch." Go to the corner across the room directly behind you. The wall that was on your left when you started in the first corner now should be on your right. (See (2) in Fig. 9-12.)

Follow the technique just described for hooking the carpet on at this new position, but use a great deal more force as you strike the kicker. You can strike the kicker several times in each position. Each time you do you force the carpet onto the tackless that much more. The carpet will stretch across the room and become much more imbedded on the tackless behind you. And, as it advances onto the tackless under you, it will stretch that much more. Check occasionally to be sure the carpet has not come off the tackless behind you.

A rule of thumb is that for every 12 feet of jute-backed carpet you can expect to get about 1 inch of stretch. That means that if you start with 2 inches of waste riding up the wall, you will have 3 inches when you have finished stretching at each point. But don't count on this. Some carpets have more stretch than others. Also, certain carpet backs require less stretching than others. The Action-Bac, for instance, requires less stretching than the jute. To test whether you have stretched your carpet enough, go to the middle of the room between the two points you have just stretched, take hold of the nap of the carpet between your thumb and forefinger, and pull up. If it feels rather loose, you probably need to stretch it some more. If it feels tight (hard to pull up), it probably is stretched enough.

After this first stretch has been accomplished, it is time to hook the carpet onto the tackless along the wall extending between the two points you have just finished. (See (3) in Fig. 9-12.) Continue kicking and tucking, using moderate strokes.

During this step you have kicked the carpet along the wall which is at 90 degrees to the first two walls you started on. Once this wall is fastened, go to the center of the opposite wall (see (4) in Fig. 9-12). Now kick the carpet onto the tackless at this point with force in order to stretch it onto the tackless. Continue this process, working at an angle toward one of the corners (whichever you prefer). (See (4a) in Fig. 9-12.) The angle causes the carpet to move toward the corner as well as toward the wall you are facing. When you get to the corner, return to the center and work in the opposite direction toward the other corner. (See (4B) Fig. 9-12.)

You now have the carpet completely stretched onto the tackless along two opposite walls. Now return to where you started and hook the carpet on along that entire wall. (See (5) Fig. 9-12.) At this point moderate strokes will do. Once this is done, go to the opposite and last wall and stretch the carpet on with heavier blows. (See (6) Fig. 9-12.) When doing these last two walls be careful that each blow is made at a 90-degree angle to the wall. If you kick at any other angle the carpet will tend to move in the direction the kicker is pointing as well as onto the tackless, and bubbles may form between each kick.

When you have finished stretching your carpet, it will be hooked onto all of the tackless around the entire room and folded into the space between the tackless and baseboard with the excess carpet flat against the baseboard. It will look very similar to a foam-backed carpet which has been ironed in.

The point of all this is to get your carpet stretched evenly over the entire room. Any stretching pattern you can create that will accomplish this is perfectly all right. Different rooms sometimes require different approaches. There is usually more than one way to stretch a room. For instance, in Fig. 9-12 you can use the following pattern.

Start as we did before, stretching between points 1 and 2 in Fig. 9-12. Then stretch from point 1 to corner A with the kicker pointing at an angle aiming toward corner A. Next, kick from point 2 to corner B with the kicker at an angle pointing toward B. Then stretch the carpet onto the tackless along wall number 4 with the kicker pointing straight toward the wall—not at an angle.

When you point the kicker at an angle, you force the carpet in both the direction of the wall you are stretching toward and the corner where you are heading. Therefore, the carpet is stretched in both directions. A bubble will develop in front of the kicker as you move along. This is the stretch you have taken out of the carpet as you progress toward the corner. It will disappear once you hook the carpet onto the tackless at the corner. Your final stretch must be made straight toward the wall, not angled toward the corner, or you will create a new bubble as you approach each corner where the carpet is already hooked on. You can end up following a bubble all around the room if you don't make your final stretch straight onto the final wall.

**Fig. 9-13** Special trimming tools are available for tackless installations.

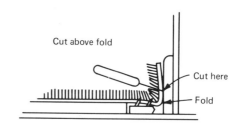

**Fig. 9-14** Trim above the fold.

The next step is to trim away all the waste, and tuck the edges of the carpet into the space left between the tackless and baseboard. Special tools for this phase of the job are available (see Fig. 9-15). They have the advantage of enabling you to trim away the right amount of carpet while protecting your baseboards from the knife blade. However, trimming tools are expensive and require a little practice before you can use them to trim the carpet correctly. While most of the professionals have trimming tools, they usually trim freehand with a knife. This, too, requires a little practice, but, after you have trimmed a few feet you will get the hang of it and move right along. The chances are that the nap of your carpet will hide most damage done to the baseboard by the knife.

When trimming for tackless installation you must make a cut that leaves ⅛ to ¼ of an inch of the back of the carpet riding up the baseboard (the amount depends on the overall thickness of the back and face yarn combined) so that when you tuck it into the space behind the tackless it will bind and not tend to come back out. This means you must cut above the fold left by your tucking tool.

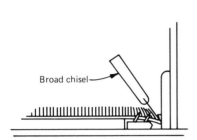

**Fig. 9-15** Tuck remainder into gap between tackless and baseboard.

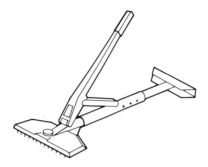

**Fig. 9-16** Power stretchers are available for difficult stretching jobs or to be certain carpet is stretched sufficiently. Many installers use them on all installations.

Starting in a corner of the room, make a short cut from the top, cutting through to the baseboard. Pull away the waste and tuck the remainder into the space with your tucking tool. If it looks neat and does not tend to come back out, then you have cut it correctly.

If you have a hard time jamming the remainder down and it tends to bend back, exposing the edge, you have cut it too long. Reach down into the space with the point of your knife and trim away some more of the excess until it looks the way you want it.

If you cut it too short, don't despair. Take your kicker and kick some more carpet onto the tackless. Chances are you can kick it on until it is where it should be for proper tucking.

Pretty soon you will discover how best to trim your carpet, and you will be able to proceed around the room. When you have finished you should have a nice, neat, tight installation with no bubbles. Sometimes trimming and tucking the carpet can create bubbles in front of the tackless. This should only require a little more kicking to move the carpet a little farther onto the tackless. Since the carpet has been tucked in already, it will probably move right on over the tackless and down into the space behind the tackless, with no further trimming and tucking. If it doesn't, then trim away a little more and retuck.

There is another tool available to you if you have a particularly heavy or stiff carpet to work with. This is called a *power stretcher*. The power stretcher is a very heavy, cumbersome, and expensive tool, but it can stretch carpet where the kicker can't. It consists of a head just like a kicker's, only

about four times as large. Behind the head is an adjustable shaft which can extend across most rooms. At the other end is a foot that rests against the baseboard opposite the point toward which you are stretching. Just behind the head there is a lever with a self-locking device that creates a mechanical force (far exceeding that which you can produce with your knee) by pushing against the baseboard at the other end of the room. Using this in place of the kicker or as an adjunct to it, you can stretch your carpet following the same pattern and technique described earlier for the kicker.

If you do use a power stretcher, be very careful where you place its foot. Be sure it is pushing against a stable wall, otherwise you can damage the wall. Be sure that the studs hidden in the wall are bridged with something more substantial (a piece of 2 x 4) than plaster, or you may push a hole in the wall. A power stretcher is powerful.

## SEAMS

There are three methods for making seams in a tackless installation; sewing, gluing with latex adhesive using a fiberglass tape, and gluing with a fiberglass and thermal-plastic tape, using an iron to melt the glue. The last process is the easiest, and is most popular with the professionals. The latex adhesive process may be best for you, for while it is more time-consuming, it requires no special tools. Unless you are working with a woven carpet, you should not consider sewing your seams. This is a very time-consuming process, and chances are you

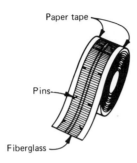

**Fig. 9-17** Fiberglass seaming tape with steel pins inserted to reinforce latex adhesive.

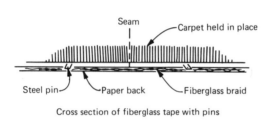

Cross section of fiberglass tape with pins

**Fig. 9-18** Cross section shows fiberglass tape with pins as it will look after seam is made.

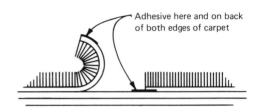

**Fig. 9-19** One-half of tape is placed under the carpet edge, the other half is ready to receive the edge which has been folded back.

**Fig. 9-20** Special iron is required for use with thermal plastic seam tape. (Courtesy Roberts Consolidated Industries.)

will not produce a seam that will stand up to the pressures of stretching.

We will start by describing the use of latex adhesive and fiberglass tape. You will need all of the usual tools, plus a small scrap of carpet about 2 by 4 inches, latex seam adhesive, and fiberglass tape purchased from your dealer for this purpose. The tape may have steel pins about every 6 inches that will add strength to your seams.

Except for fastening down the carpet, all of the preparations for making seams discussed in Chapter 7 apply here. But with a tackless installation, the seams must be made after you have rough-cut the carpet and before you have done any stretching or final trimming. The carpet should be lying in place loose with the seam edges all trimmed and butting each other.

Fold back one edge of carpet so it will be out of the way. Place your tape under the remaining edge with one-half of its width exposed so it will make contact with the edge you have folded out of the way when you replace it. Hook the tape onto the tackless at each end to help keep it from moving.

Now fold back the remaining edge of carpet. The entire tape is now exposed with the fiberglass up.

Next, apply a bead of latex adhesive approximately ½ to ¾ of an inch wide along the entire length of the tape. With a carpet scrap, spread the adhesive over all of the fiberglass but not the edges of the paper back. The paper back is there to prevent the adhesive from spilling over onto your pad, though it will not be the end of the world if it does—just wipe it up. When you have the adhesive applied to the entire tape, it should be quite wet, though not so wet that when you press your carpet in place the adhesive squeezes up into the seam or out onto the pad.

Next, with the carpet scrap, paint a thin coat of adhesive on the back of the carpet along both edges where they will make contact with the tape. (See Fig. 9-20.) Now drop one of your edges of carpet in place, leaving one-half of the fiberglass exposed. Run a bead of the same adhesive along this edge at the base of the yarn, as discussed in Chapter 7. Then drop the second edge in place, carefully, a foot or so at a time, being sure none of the adhesive gets onto the face of the carpet. If it does, wipe it away using a wet rag. As long as the adhesive stays wet it is water soluble.

The carpet edges now should be pressed onto the tape. To be sure you get good contact along the entire seam, use a hammer and gently pound the carpet onto the tape.

Now let the adhesive dry. This will take at least two hours—the longer you wait the better. Once it has set up it should be very strong. After it has thoroughly dried, you can proceed with your tackless installation as if you had one piece of carpet.

A variation on this process makes it possible to stretch your carpet first and then make the seam, thereby eliminating the need to wait for the seam to dry. To do this, lay out and rough-cut your carpet in with the edges at the seam overlapping. Now stretch each piece onto the tackless (one at a time) making your last stretch on both pieces toward the seam. Stay at least 1 foot back from the seam. As you stretch toward the seam, nail "stay tacks" (nails) into the carpet immediately in front of your kicker, leaving enough of each tack exposed so that you will be able to pull it out later. The stay tacks will hold the stretch in the carpet until your seam has been completed. Once the seam has dried, you can remove the tacks. Any puckering at the seam should recede if you really did get a good stretch in the first place. This is where a power stretcher can be very helpful, as it will hold your stretch while you place the stay tacks.

Latex adhesive and fiberglass tape were used by the professionals until thermal-plastic tape was created. Seams made using thermal-plastic tape involve basically the same process but with much less mess and fuss. And the carpet will be ready for stretching about ten minutes after the seam has been made. A special iron is used to melt the tape, enabling it to stick to the carpet. (See Fig. 9-20.) You will probably have to rent the iron from a dealer.

Thermal-plastic tape (heat tape) is a fiberglass tape with a paper back and surface layer of very stiff glue that has to be melted as you make your seam. The process is as follows.

First, plug in your iron and set it aside. Be sure it is resting on its protective platform and not directly on the carpet. Set the temperature no higher than 250 degrees. (A higher setting could damage the yarns.) Next, lay out the carpet as has been described, with one of the edges folded back. Place your tape with the plastic adhesive up and halfway under the carpet edge that remains on the floor (as in Fig. 9-19 showing latex tape). Now run your bead of latex adhesive at the base of the yarn along one edge, lifting the carpet off the tape as you go along to avoid getting the latex on the heat tape. Now drop the second edge in place carefully, so that the edges butt exactly.

When the iron has heated (a little light will indicate when it has reached the right temperature) take hold of it with one hand, leaving the safety platform near the end of the seam where you will be finishing. Starting at the other end, pull the carpet edges back so that you can insert the iron without touching them. Place the iron on the tape and let it heat the plastic for ten to fifteen seconds. Once the melting process has started, push the iron along the tape a few inches at a time. Press the carpet edges together and into the heat tape behind the iron as it moves along. Have the kicker at hand so that you can gently move the edges back and forth to be sure they butt and do not leave a gap or overlap.

Do not rush with the iron. It needs time to melt the plastic. Look behind the iron from time to time to be sure the plastic is melting properly. The iron should move smoothly. If the iron drags, the plastic is probably not melted enough.

As you place the edges together, use a heavy box such as a tool box to press the carpet into the melted adhesive and flatten the surface to prevent curling. Move the box along following the iron. Otherwise, the carpet may pucker up or curl while the tape is cooling. This normally comes out with stretching, but the heavy tool box will keep it to a minimum. Some installers use a piece of corrugated cardboard or thin piece of plywood to help prevent curling. They place the board under the tape where the iron is resting. Then they move the board along as they move the iron. This insulates the pad from the heat and provides a flat surface for the tape to conform to as it begins to cool.

Another technique to ensure a flat surface is to make the seams on the subfloor before the pad is installed. But this can become quite cumbersome when the carpet has to be folded out of the way in order to install the pad.

In any case, about ten minutes after you have finished making your seam you will be able to go ahead with your installation.

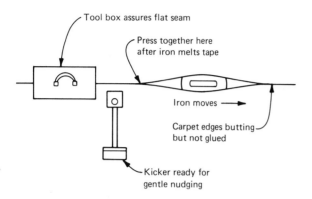

**Fig. 9-21** To ensure minimum of puckering move tool box along behind iron after you are sure carpet edges are butting properly.

When installing a thermal-plastic-seamed carpet, try to plan the stretch so that you will be exerting a maximum of force across the seam. This will help to eliminate any puckering which may have occurred in the heat tape. Also, when joining two rooms of carpet at a doorway, try to make sure that at least one of the stretches in one of the rooms will pull away from that door after the seam has been made. Otherwise, you may end up with some looseness at the door.

## STAIRS

Installing carpet wall to wall on stairs with tackless is similar to installing it in a room. Each riser and tread equals a room and must have tackless installed on it. Then pad is installed inside the tackless, and the carpet is installed stretching from one edge to its opposite. The technique is as follows.

First, install the tackless. Put one strip across the treads approximately ½ of an inch out from the riser with the pins pointing toward the riser. Put other strips on either end of the treads at 90-degree angles to the first strip, and running from the first strip to within about ½ of an inch of the nosing. As in a room, place these strips about ¼ to ⅜ of an inch from the wall. The pins must face their respective walls as they would in a room installation. Next, install a piece of tackless near the bottom of each of the risers. It should extend to within 1 to 1½ inches of the ends of the risers. This strip should be installed with its edge about 1 to 1½

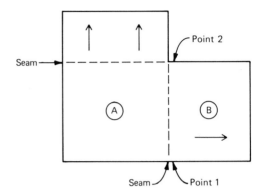

**Fig. 9-22** When stretching maximum force should be in direction of arrows across seams. In the above illustration you might make up and install room A first, letting carpet drop into the doorway. Next spread room B. Hook carpet at point 1 and stretch to point 2. Now both carpets have been stretched along the common wall between the two rooms. Hook room B carpet on along this wall and make a seam in the doorway. Next stretch across room B away from doorway seam.

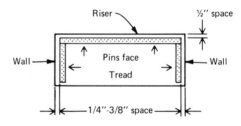

**Fig. 9-23** Placement of tackless on stair tread.

inches above the tread below and with the pins pointing down toward that same tread.

Next, install the pad. Cut individual pieces which will fit between the tackless strips at each end of the treads and which will extend from the strip on the riser over the nosing to the corresponding strip on the tread above. Staple the pad around its edges, including those on the riser.

The stairs are now ready to receive the carpet. Unlike a room installation, the carpet to be installed on the stairs should be close to exactly the width desired. If there is more than a net fit—especially across the risers—you are likely to end up with bubbles. In addition, trimming-in carpet in the confining area of stairs can be difficult. If your stairs are straight and have the same width at the top stair as at the bottom, you can cut out a runner which will be exactly the width needed. Roll it up in

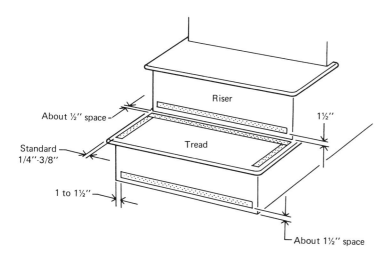

**Fig. 9-24** Placement of tackless on stairs ready to receive a pad.

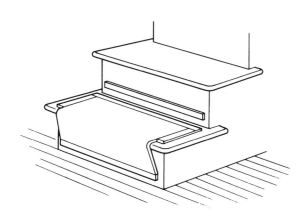

**Fig. 9-25** The pad is installed inside tackless nad pulled over nosing down to just above tackless on lower riser, then stapled.

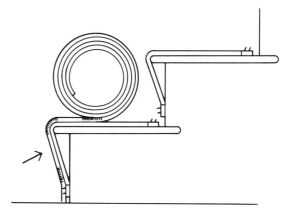

**Fig. 9-26** Force carpet, which is a bit too long, in at arrow. Apply a few tacks to make sure it will stay in place.

the manner described for the glue-down installation. (See Chapter 8.) Place the end of the carpet at the foot of the stairs so that it is properly placed between the walls. See that as the carpet unrolls it will stay properly placed as it continues up the stairs. Be sure it does not head off at a disturbing angle.

Now press the back of the carpet onto the first piece of tackless on the first riser. Have the strip of carpet filling the space below this tackless a bit long (perhaps ⅛ of an inch). Then as you force the carpet into that space it will be forced onto the pins and tend to stay there. You may need to put in a few carpet tacks below this first piece of tackless to make sure the carpet stays on.

Next, unroll the carpet up over the first tread and up the next riser. Let the roll rest on the second tread. With your hands, press it onto the next piece of tackless on the first tread. Once you have the first tread placed to your satisfaction, take your kicker in hand. Place the head immediately behind the tackless on the tread in the center. Strike the kicker with your knee. This will force the carpet to stretch from the tackless on the riser below to the tackless on the tread. Continue this action, working toward each end of the tread. When you have finished, the carpet should be hooked on very tight and flat. If there is some bubbling on the riser it may mean the carpet is a bit too wide. Remove it and cut away a little. Some-

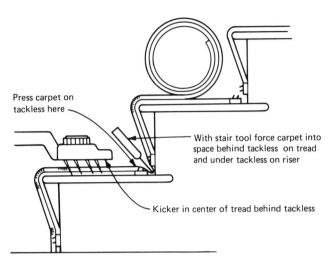

Press carpet on
tackless here

With stair tool force carpet into
space behind tackless on tread
and under tackless on riser

Kicker in center of tread behind tackless

**Fig. 9-27** Placement of kicker for stretching carpet
onto tread. Carpet is tucked with stair tool as shown after
it has been kicked on.

times ⅛ of an inch can make a great deal of
difference. Any bubbling on the tread can be
removed by kicking the carpet onto the tackless at
each end of the tread and tucking it in. Do this
even if there are no bubbles.

Once the first tread is installed, take the broad
chisel (a special stair tool, Fig. 7-2, has been
designed for this purpose) and force the carpet
down into the space behind the tackless running
across the back of this tread. (See Fig. 9-7.) This
action will also force the carpet onto the tackless on
the next riser. Once you have the carpet well
tucked so that there is a real fold at this point, you
can proceed to the next tread in the same manner.
Once you have mastered the technique you will
find that this type of installation goes in very
quickly.

If you are putting a runner on the steps the
technique is basically the same. In this case, install
the tackless on the treads and risers as has been
described, but eliminate the end pieces on the
treads and cut the tackless about 3 inches less than
the width desired for the carpet. Install the pad as
has been described, but keep the width of the
pieces the same as the tackless. When the carpet is
installed, the finished edges will overlap the tackless and pad by 1½ inches on each side. This will
prevent the underpinnings from showing.

If the carpet edges are bound, the runner can
be installed in exactly the same manner. There
should be no bubbling problem (unless an uneven
stretch has been made), since there will be no walls
to interfere with the edges of the carpet, and it
should go on very easily. If the carpet is not bound,
the edges probably will need to be folded under as
described in Chapter 8.

If you have a particularly complicated staircase with winders and all sorts of different measurements, then each tread may have to be installed separately. All of the installation principles
apply, but you won't be able to cut each piece
exactly to fit and you will have to work a bit harder
trimming each piece just as you would in a room.

Finally, the judicious use of a few carpet tacks
here and there can help rescue a situation where
you just don't seem to be able to get the carpet to
go in exactly right. The professionals have very
expensive electric tackers which they employ quite
liberally at times for this purpose. It will take you
longer using a hammer and tacks, but the principle
is the same.

## UPHOLSTERING

When planning to upholster steps, you should
follow the installation instructions given for wall to
wall. However, you will have to cut your stair
runners so that they will be wide enough to extend
through the rungs of the banister and around the
ends of the treads. Refer to the sections in Chapter
8 on upholstering.

# 10 Installing Linoleum

Today linoleum manufacturers are making great strides toward helping the do-it-yourselfer. The mills are producing cushioned linoleums that are relatively simple to work with. All kinds of brochures have been produced illustrating how to install these products. Armstrong's Interflex system linoleums are incredibly easy to handle.

## FREEHANDING

Most of today's do-it-yourself linoleums and *some* inlaid vinyls can be installed much the same way as a foam-backed carpet. This is called *freehanding*, and usually requires that you work with the softer, cushioned floor materials.

Assume that your subfloor is ready for linoleum (see Chapter 6), and that appropriate metal trims have been installed in doorways. (See Chapter 13.) Also assume that your linoleum is going into the room in one piece. Seams will be discussed later.

You have a roll of material that is slightly larger than the widest and longest dimensions of the room. Linoleum, unlike carpet, is rolled with the top side out. Therefore, you must be careful not to scratch the surface when unwrapping it and getting it spread out on the floor. When unrolling linoleum it must be at room temperature.

Once you have the material spread out it will be riding up each of the walls a few inches, waiting to be trimmed to a net fit. You may need to rough-cut it if the room has an irregular shape. This is done exactly as with carpet (see Chapter 8). But be more careful with your initial handling of the material. Do not let kinks develop in it, as these can damage the goods. (Although some of Armstrong's Interflex floors can be folded like a blanket.) Never pull hard on the material. Be gentle with it. If the piece gets stuck, stop and find out what's holding it back. Tugging at it could cause a tear. If you are working with a large piece, you had better have someone help you get it spread out. Once you have it spread and rough-cut, with all large areas of waste cut away, you will be ready for the next step.

This next step depends on whether and how you are going to fasten the floor down. If your linoleum is to be loose-laid or fastened around the edges, your next step is trimming it in. If it is to be cemented all over, your next step is to spread the cement. It is especially important to know the manufacturer's recommendations regarding how your floor can be fastened down, as no guarantees will be valid if you do not follow their instructions. Do not loose-lay your linoleum or fasten it only around the edges unless you are sure the manufacturer says you can. Many installers tell me that, no matter what the manufacturer says, they cement all over. They are concerned that otherwise the floor may bubble up later—no matter what the manufacturer may say. However, you must be certain the manufacturer will approve cementing all over. Armstrong's Interflex floors specifically call for cementing edges only.

## CEMENTING ALL OVER

In any case, assume that cementing is your next step. First, be sure your floor is dust free. Next, fold back your material so that you have exposed half of the floor. Be sure you do not let a kink develop, and do not step on the fold. Do not, for example, use the technique described in Chapter 8 for folding foam-backed carpet. Some linoleums are more "forgiving" than others in this respect, but you can damage them if you are not careful.

Now spread the cement. Be sure the adhesive is recommended for use under your floor, and follow the directions on the label regarding the size notched trowel to be used and other application procedures. See Chapter 8 for detailed cement-spreading techniques.

Once you have covered the first half of your floor, put the linoleum back down. Make sure it lies flat. Roll this half to make sure that the linoleum makes contact with the adhesive over every square inch of the floor. Next, fold back the other half of the room, apply the cement, replace the linoleum and roll it. The professionals have special rollers for this purpose. If you can obtain one, then use it. Roll the floor across the room and lengthwise, so that each pass over the floor overlaps the previous one. If, however, you cannot get a roller, you can use a push broom. Push it before you as you would the roller, but bear down so that you apply pressure to the floor. Be sure to use a soft-bristled brush and let only the bristles touch the linoleum. After you have rolled (or brushed) the first half, pull back and cement the second half and roll it. One caution; many all-purpose latex adhesives become very sticky once firm contact is made. Therefore, you should avoid walking on your floor before you are sure it is lying flat. Otherwise, a bubble could form in front of the roller which you might not be able to push forward beyond the point where you have stepped.

Sometimes bubbles show up in the floor even after it has been completely stuck down. They may

**Fig. 10-1** Rollers, such as Crain's shown above, come in varying weights, usually 75 to 100 lbs. (Courtesy Crain Cutter Co. Inc.)

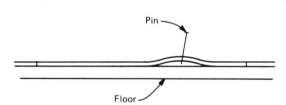

**Fig. 10-2** If bubble persists in your linoleum, puncture it with a pin. Then seal puncture with vinyl weld.

even appear several hours later. This condition is usually caused by an overly generous application of adhesive. The adhesive emits gases while drying that are unable to escape through the nonporous surface as fast as they are produced, developing a bubble. These bubbles should go down in time. As long as contact was made with the adhesive initially, the linoleum should stick permanently once its back comes in contact with the floor again. If a bubble persists, you can use a straight pin to puncture it and let the gas escape. The puncture should have a drop of seam sealer applied to it after the gas escapes (see the section on Seams).

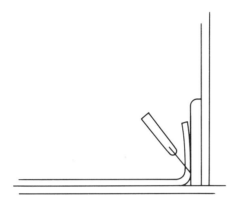

**Fig. 10-3** Cut higher than fold with blade at angle shown.

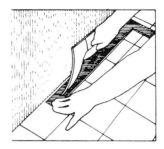

**Fig. 10-4** Armstrong suggests using a carpenter's square as an aid to trimming. (Courtesy Armstrong Cork Co.)

Now that your floor is cemented and rolled, you are ready to trim it in. Freehanding is a process of trial and error. The trick, therefore, is to be sure that any error you make is in your favor.

Start in the corner of the room which is least important to you. Iron your material in as you would a cemented carpet (see Chapter 8). But be very gentle with this process. Just try to get the material to conform to the floor and baseboard as best you can without damaging it. If you cannot get a real crease, don't worry about it. The ironing-in is only to give you an idea where your knife should be used. You may only be able to iron-in a foot or so at a time before trimming because the material may spring back into a curve where it meets the baseboard.

While you do have some sort of a crease, apply your knife to the goods at a point considerably *higher* than where you think a net fit will occur. Chances are the material will be too long when you pull away the waste, but this will give you a clue as to where you should be heading. Now cut away a little more and keep trimming away, checking after each cut, until the material drops into place.

When trimming, hold the knife so that the blade is pressed against the baseboard at a 45 degree angle to the floor (see Fig. 10-3). This will create a bevel in your cut, and more of the back than the top of the goods will be cut away. When you get close to having a net fit you will find that most of what's left to be trimmed is the wear layer. This will trim away very neatly.

The professionals are able to freehand linoleum with only one or two trims. Chances are,

by the time you have completed the perimeter of your room, you too will be making many fewer cuts than when you started.

A variation of this trimming procedure is suggested by Armstrong in their literature on trimming-in Tredway floors. They suggest using a carpenter's square to hold the linoleum in an ironed-in position while you trim. The square lies flat on the floor pressed into the crease with its edge against the baseboard. You then cut the linoleum holding your knife at a 45-degree angle, using the edge of the square as a guide. The success you have with this procedure will depend on how thick and how stiff the product is.

## FASTENING AROUND THE EDGES

Armstrong's Interflex floors specifically require only a "perimifloor" installation. The manufacturer claims that cementing all over is unnecessary. Therefore, the Interflex floors can be installed over almost any surface, and tolerate a less perfect subfloor than do materials that require cementing all over. In addition, Armstrong says these floors have a "desire" to shrink. They must be fastened at the edges within two hours of trimming. The tendency to shrink gives them the additional feature of self-smoothing, should you be left with a few minor bubbles after installation. This last feature is not foolproof. Do not assume that bubbles will disappear. But, if you have made every effort to get the floor to lie flat and a few bubbles persist, they probably will disappear within a day or so.

**Fig. 10-5** Sometimes a staple gun can be used for perimifloor installations. (Courtesy Armstrong Cork Co.)

The shrinkage factor can also cause the material to pull away from the edges and seams if not fastened securely. You must use Armstrong's materials exclusively, exactly following their directions, for installing these products. Another feature of the Interflex floors is that, should you cut the floor a bit too short, you can stretch it back to where you wish you had trimmed it.

Finally, if you can install the baseboards after the linoleum, you can staple the material about every 3 inches around the edges with a staple gun.

Many other floors presently on the market have some, if not all, of these features. Undoubtedly more will be introduced which will include all. Just be sure, before you try to take advantage of them, that the manufacturer guarantees their product meets your requirements.

If you are going to fasten your goods around the edges only, do your final trim first, then fasten the goods. Instead of pulling your material back uncovering half of the floor, you will only pull it back enough to apply the adhesive over a few inches of the floor. If stapling it, don't pull it back at all. When using adhesive be sure you use one specified by the linoleum manufacturer. In some instances special contact adhesives are required.

## LOOSE LAY

I do not recommend loose laying any good quality linoleum. No matter what the manufacturers say,

there simply is too much opportunity for edges to curl up, get tripped over, and break, as well as for bubbles to develop as the years go by. I feel the same way about fastening at the edges only, with the exception of the Interflex floors. Cementing the floor is not that big a job nor that expensive when you consider the problems you may prevent.

If you are going to loose-lay your goods—some of the really cheap goods don't last long and are not worth cementing—then your next step, after spreading the goods and rough-cutting, is to make the final trim. You should consider using double-faced tape at doors and along seams (as described in Chapter 8 for loose-lay carpet installations).

## PATTERN SCRIBING

Until the softer vinyls came on the market, pattern scribing was the only way to install linoleum. Generally speaking, inlays should be scribed. Freehanding is too dangerous, as these stiffer goods break very easily. The very name *pattern scribing* scares many a person away. To many this is strictly for the professionals. But the principle is quite simple. The execution takes a bit of practice, but I have seen many a novice do his/her first pattern only to be amazed at how beautifully the material went in.

Pattern scribing is a process by which you create, on a piece of paper, a pattern which exactly duplicates all of the ins and outs of the perimeter of the room. You transfer this pattern to the goods to be installed in the room. Then trim the material down to the actual size of the room, with all its ins and outs, before you bring it into the room. Then apply adhesive to the floor, and stick the linoleum down with little or no trimming. Here's what you will need.

First, this process requires a space (not the room) with a firm floor larger than the piece of linoleum to be scribed.

Second, you need some sort of very stiff paper on which the pattern can be scribed. I recommend flooring felt. There are several flooring felts available, made by the linoleum manufacturers. Do not use roofing felt. It may look the same and be less expensive but it will not act the same. It is important that the pattern material not expand, or

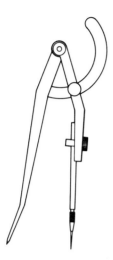

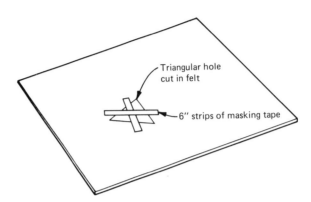

**Fig. 10-6** Specially designed scribing tools, such as Crain's shown above, are available. (Courtesy Crain Cutter Co. Inc.)

**Fig. 10-7** Felt can be fastened with masking tape applied across a triangle cut out as shown above.

shrink, or move around in any way, or your pattern will not be accurately transferred to the linoleum.

Third, you need a scribing tool. Special tools are available—some are relatively inexpensive. But, if you are not going to be working too large an area, a pencil compass will do. You can also use a straightedge such as a short ruler. It should be 1½ to 2 inches wide.

You'll also need your knife (new blade), adhesive, notched trowel, and some masking tape.

Here's how you scribe a pattern. First be sure the floor is ready for the linoleum—clean, dust and bump free. Unroll the flooring felt across the room, cutting off lengths which will reach from wall to wall. If your room is 9 by 12 feet, you'll need four 9-foot-long pieces (4 × 3-foot-wide material = 12 feet). Place your pieces side by side with the edges butting at the seams. (Do not overlap.) Fasten the felt to the floor so it can't move while you are scribing your pattern. You can accomplish this by cutting triangles out of the center of each piece of felt, exposing the floor underneath. The legs of each triangle can be 2 or 3 inches long. Put 6-inch-long pieces of masking tape across the open triangles so that the tape sticks the felt to the floor underneath. Three triangles in each strip of felt will prevent movement of the felt.

Now set your scribing tool (compass) so that you have about 2 inches between the two points

(point and pencil). The actual distance is not important as long as it *does not change* during this entire process—this is very important. Now number each sheet of felt (1, 2, 3, etc.). Next, run some lines across the seams of the felt at various points, using your scriber. This ensures that when you take the felt up from the floor and later put it down on the linoleum these lines will correspond and you will get the sheets in place as they were on the floor.

Now trim the felt in at any place where it is riding up the walls. Leave about ½ of an inch of subfloor exposed all around the edges of the room.

Now you are ready to scribe your pattern. Starting on a relatively straight wall, place one point of the compass against the baseboard, touching the floor and baseboard. Place the other point (pencil) on the felt. Think of an imaginary straight line which extends between the two points. Keep this line at a 90-degree angle to the wall at all times. Now draw the scribing tool along the wall keeping the one point against the baseboard and the other on the felt at that 90-degree angle. As you move along, the first point will go in and out with the ins and outs of the wall and the other point (pencil) will scribe (draw) a line on the felt matching this pattern. When you come to a corner (even on door trim) turn the scriber in exactly the same direction as the corner turns, maintaining the 90-degree angle. If it is an inside corner, the lines you scribe

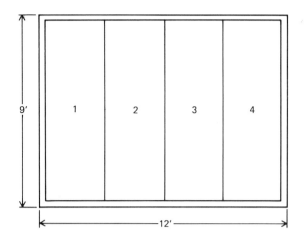

**Fig. 10-8** Scratch a number (1, 2, 3 etc.) on sheets of felt to help keep track of which goes where.

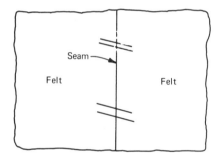

**Fig. 10-9** Scratch lines in felt at joints. These will match after you put them together again on top of linoleum.

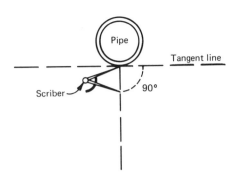

**Fig. 10-10** Keep imaginary line between points of scriber at 90 degrees to surface being scribed.

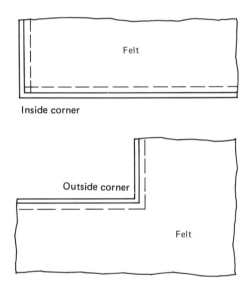

**Fig. 10-11** Dotted line equals scribe line. Lines intersect at inside corner. Lines do not touch with outside corners.

on the felt will intersect each other. If it is an outside corner they will not intersect but will be several inches apart where they end, depending on the distance between the points of the scriber. Don't let this worry you. The lines will come back together when you transfer the pattern to the linoleum. This process works no matter what you are scribing. You can go around pipes, toilets, door-jambs, and other protrusions. Just keep those two points the same distance apart and 90 degrees to the edge you are scribing, no matter how short that edge is.

Now spread out your linoleum where you will be able to work on it. It should be on a firm, clean

surface such as a garage floor. Next take up your felt, being careful not to let is rip or kink or in any way lose its basic dimensions. Lay it out on the linoleum, making sure that all the lines you scribed across the seams of the felt match. Place the masking tape across the triangles again, fastening the felt to the linoleum.

Now you are ready to transfer the pattern to the linoleum. Place the point of the compass which was against the baseboard onto the line you have scribed on the felt. Place the other point (pencil) on the linoleum. Keeping the line between the points at a 90-degree angle to the line you scribed on the felt, draw your scriber along so that a line is scribed

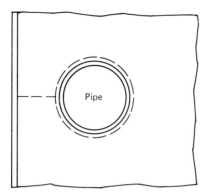

**Fig. 10-12** Scribe line from pipe to most convenient edge.

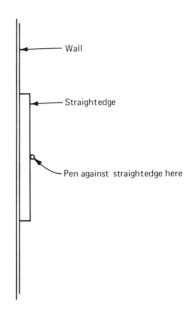

**Fig. 10-13** Often a straightedge can be used for scribing.

(drawn) on the linoleum. Faithfully follow each and every line you scribed onto the felt, and you will see the outline of your room reproduced on the linoleum. Where you have scribed pipes, posts, toilets, and other items which stick up out of the middle of the floor, you will have to run an additional line to the most convenient edge of the linoleum. You will have to cut along this line to the outline of the pipe, etc., so that you can install the material around it.

Once you have faithfully scribed every line from the felt to the linoleum you can cut the material along this line. When you have cut all the waste away you will have a piece of linoleum that looks like and exactly fits into your room.

I mentioned earlier that you can use a straightedge instead of a special scribing tool or compass. The procedure is the same. Place one edge of the straightedge against the wall and the other on the felt. Then place a ball-point pen or other scriber against the straightedge on the felt. Draw the two along the wall with the pen drawing a line on the felt. The advantage of using a straightedge is that there is no chance the interval between the two edges will change, as it can between the two points of a compass. The disadvantage is that a straightedge may not fit into every nook and cranny of the room. Some installers use both—the straightedge for the straight walls and the scriber for more complicated areas.

You are now ready to cement the floor. This may require a strategy session with yourself to figure out how you can pull one-half of the linoleum back and get the adhesive down, then pull the other half back. With all the waste out of the way, you will find it much easier to get the goods into the room and to maneuver it. You must be careful, though, not to horse around with inlaid flooring. Treat it with respect, or it can break or tear.

Practice scribing a pattern on some dispensable material such as another piece of flooring felt or a stiff piece of paper. Or try installing a piece of the linoleum in a small closet where the results won't matter that much. Once you have scribed a pattern you'll find there's nothing quite so satisfying as seeing that piece of linoleum fit right in.

## WALL SCRIBING

Wall scribing is a variation of pattern scribing. Here you scribe the pattern directly onto the linoleum from the wall. Instead of going through the intermediate steps of putting the pattern on a piece of flooring felt and from the felt onto the goods, you lay the edge of the linoleum directly next to the wall to be trimmed, and using the scribing tool, run it along the wall scribing the pattern directly onto the linoleum. Then you trim the goods along the line scribed onto the material, after which it will fit against the wall.

This method requires very careful measuring and marking of the material to be sure that each time you scribe a wall the material will trim-in correctly in relation to the wall previously trimmed.

When you start to scribe your first wall there probably will be a portion at each end of the material which is riding up the adjacent walls waiting to be scribed and trimmed. You should trim a few inches at each of these ends to an almost net fit to enable the material to lie flat at the ends while you are scribing the wall between them. Now move your material out from this first wall so that the edge clears it enough for the material to lie flat along its entire length, but not so much that the two points of your scribing tool can't reach from the wall onto the material. Make sure, too, that you will not end up trimming so much of the material away that it will not reach to the wall behind you after you have trimmed it in to the first wall. Now scribe and trim this first wall.

Next, you must note exactly where the pattern of the material will end up in relation to the second wall. With the material in place along the first wall, mark on the baseboard of the second wall and correspondingly on your material, two or more points which, while you are making your second scribe, must stay lined up.

Next, you must determine how far out the material should be brought from the second wall for scribing. With the material still in place on the first wall, mark a line at the center of the baseboard on the first wall just trimmed and correspondingly on the linoleum. Now note the interval you have set between the points of your scribing tool. Move the goods out from the second wall until the marks on the material have moved from the marks on the baseboard this exact amount. Make sure, though, that the marks on the wall to be scribed stay lined up with their corresponding marks on the material. Now scribe and trim your second wall.

Follow the same basic procedures all the way around the room.

As you can see, the key to success with this method is very careful measuring and marking to be sure things will go back as they should. Check and recheck before making any scribes and cuts.

Also, different rooms often require different approaches to trimming. Sometimes installers will freehand three sides of a room but wall scribe the first (it may be particularly complicated). Or they might combine all three methods, pattern scribing, wall scribing, and freehanding. It all is a matter of sizing up the job properly.

## SEAMS

It is important to reiterate here that you must use installation materials designed for the floor covering you have chosen. That is the only way you can be sure the manufacturer will stand behind the product.

### Seams in Rotogravure Products

Assume that you have measured your room and ordered material for the installation knowing where the pieces are going to be placed. You are installing material which comes 6 feet wide in a room that is 6½ feet by 11 feet. You have decided to put the linoleum down in two pieces with a 6½-foot seam running across the middle of the room. Cut your first piece a bit longer than a net fit—say 6 feet 9 inches long—and spread it so that it is exactly where you want it. This will leave approximately one-half of the floor exposed. Draw a line on the floor where the seam is going to be, using the edge of the material as your guide. Now fold that piece back halfway and cement it following the instructions given earlier in this chapter. Cement only to within 1 foot of the line you drew on the floor. Then cement the other half, and roll the whole piece. The line you drew on the floor will show whether you have the piece exactly back in place as you want it. If there has been a slight shift you may be able to move the linoleum a bit by lifting it off of the adhesive (before rolling) if you act fairly quickly. This will depend on the "open time" of the cement you are using. A slight shift in the goods may not matter. You can be the judge. Now trim the edges around the three walls.

Next, place your second sheet on the floor, lining up the pattern with the first piece. The factory edge is wider than the pattern calls for, causing the pieces to overlap when you match the pattern. This is as it should be. At this point, check the manufacturer's directions about how the sheets are to be placed in relation to each other. In some cases the pattern should be run in the same direction, just as the nap in carpet should run in the same direction. This means that as you cut the

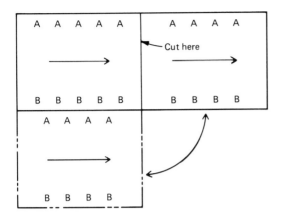

Fig. 10-14 When the roll of linoleum is cut into pieces which are laid side by side, do not reverse the direction of the pattern unless required by manufacturer. In the above pattern running in the direction of the arrows, side A goes next to side B to keep pattern running correctly.

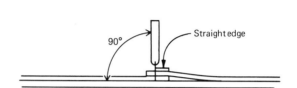

Fig. 10-16 Knife at 90-degree angle to floor. Use metal straightedge as a guide to maintain a straight cut.

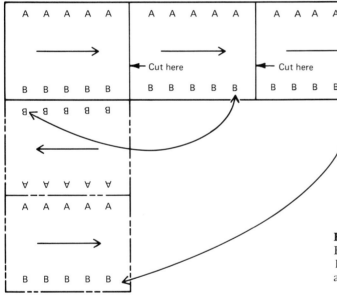

Fig. 10-15 To reverse sheets, edge B goes against edge B and edge A goes against edge A. Thus pattern changes 180 degrees as each successive piece is cut off the roll and placed next to the previous place.

material off the roll and place the sheets on the floor, you always keep the same edge parallel to the same wall. If the two edges are labeled A and B, edge A joins edge B as the two sheets are put side by side.

Sometimes the manufacturer instructs that the sheets be reversed. This is usually indicated on the edge of the material with the words *reverse sheets,* and each edge is lettered so that you'll know which is which. This means that, for example, edge A

should be joined to edge A. The second sheet is turned 180 degrees before it is placed next to the first sheet.

If you do not lay the sheets facing in the proper directions, your linoleum may seem to be two different colors, even though it came off the same roll.

Once you have your second piece placed with the pattern matched, cement and trim it in just as you did the first. Be sure to apply adhesive only to within 1 foot of the seam. Cement the seam half first to allow shifting if necessary.

You now are ready to trim the seam in. With most rotogravure products this is done by "double cutting" the seam. With a very sharp knife held perfectly straight up and down, cut through both layers of your overlapping material at the same time. If possible follow a "grout line" in the pattern. Use some sort of straightedge (carpenter's square) to maintain a straight line and keep your knife from wandering away from where you want the seam. Do not allow your knife to curve in its travels along the cut. Keep your strokes as straight as possible. Straight lines made through two layers of linoleum match up better than curved cuts. Once you have completed your double cut, pull out the pieces of overlap you have cut off. Your two edges should match.

Now is the time to apply adhesive under your seam. Some linoleums require special seam adhesives (different from the adhesive applied over most of the floor). The flooring material involved may curl up at the seams later on if special seam adhesive is not used. This is the time to apply such an adhesive. Some manufacturers do not recommend special seam adhesives, and may even instruct you to apply your basic adhesive along seam areas when you cement the rest of the floor. They assume that when you pull out the little piece of waste the two edges will fall into place and be held securely by the adhesive remaining. They don't think the small amount taken away on the back of the waste you have pulled out is enough to matter. I feel, however, that the edges at the seam may not hold in these circumstances, and that you should wait until you have trimmed your seam in before applying adhesive under it, even if you are going to use the same adhesive. This creates an extra step, but it will ensure a good seam.

Once you have finished trimming and cementing the seam, clean away any adhesive which may have seeped up through the new joint.

The next step is to seal or "weld" the seam. Most rotogravure products require welding. The dealer can supply you with the solution and applicator needed for your floor. Usually the applicator consists of a small plastic bottle with a special nozzle. The nozzle has a tiny hole in it just above a little fin. This fin is inserted into the seam at one end and acts as a guide as you pull the applicator along the seam, allowing the solution to

come out through the hole and down into the seam. You control the flow of the solution by applying pressure to the bottle. A bead of solution about ⅛ of an inch wide should be applied along the entire length of the seam. This bead may be very visible when first applied—more so than the seam itself. Don't worry, it will wear off, leaving a seam with edges welded together. This is just about as close as you can get to having a seamless floor with more than one piece. This welding process is not always perfect, and it may fail occasionally, but it is a tremendous improvement over no welding at all.

## Seams in Loose-Lay Installations

All seams should be fastened down in any proper installation including loose lay—unless you just don't care. With loose-lay installation it is simpler to cement the seams first and then trim the walls in. In this way the material will not shift and destroy your pattern match at the seam while you are trimming the walls.

Other than this precaution, seams are made as described for cemented floors. One further simplification would be to use double-faced tape under the edges at the seams rather than adhesive. But, be sure the manufacturer of your goods says double-faced tape will be all right.

## Seams in Inlaid Products

Most inlaid linoleums require pattern scribing. To properly seam your inlaid floor you must first install one piece using all the pattern scribing instructions given in this chapter. With the first piece in place, spread your flooring felt and make the pattern for the second piece. This procedure is no different from scribing a one-piece room, except that you must carefully mark your felt at the point where the seam is going to occur and make special marks to indicate where the pattern should match. To facilitate pattern matching between the pieces, choose an easily recognized point on the pattern near the center of the first piece, and mark a corresponding spot on the felt. When you carry the felt over to the sheet to be trimmed, look for that point in the pattern on the second sheet and line it up directly beneath the spot on the felt.

Now scribe your pattern onto the three edges of the linoleum that will go against the three walls

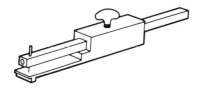

**Fig. 10-17** An underscribing tool will be needed for most inlaid seams. (Courtesy Beno J. Gundlach Co.)

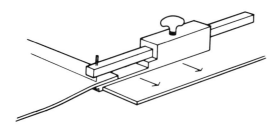

**Fig. 10-18** The underscriber uses a pre-trimmed edge underneath as a guide to scribe matching edge on top.

of the room. Next, using a straightedge and a very sharp knife, trim away the edge where the seam is to be, leaving only the amount required to make a proper match with the piece already installed. The edge you leave will be used as a guide for trimming off the piece already in place on the floor. You can reverse this process if you wish, and trim the edge of the first piece installed, then use this as a guide for trimming the second piece. You are *not* going to double cut your seam.

When you place the second piece you will find the two pieces overlap at the seam. Place the trimmed edge underneath. Now you will need a special "underscribing" tool. It is not particularly expensive. A guide on the tool follows the edge underneath while a needle on top scribes a line exactly matching what the guide tells it.

Cement your second piece, being careful that you do not lose the pattern match. Now, using your underscriber, scribe the line for trimming the second edge. Following this line with your knife and straightedge, cut away the excess. When the two trimmed edges fall into place they will go together. In following this last instruction you must be very careful. The underscribing tool is adjustable. Before scribing the seam you must make certain that the needle truly does scribe exactly

over the line of the edge of the linoleum which is underneath. Even after you have determined that it does, you should first scribe only a short section of seam, then trim this away and let it fall into place. If it comes together correctly then the rest of the seam should be all right. Otherwise you will have to adjust the needle until it gives you a proper line.

Now cement under the seam, using a special adhesive if it is called for. Then clean the seam and carefully remove any burrs that the scribe might have left, using a very light application of steel wool.

Finally, seal the seam (as and if required by the manufacturer) as has been described.

## HINTS AND CORRECTING MISTAKES

Suppose, after all is done, you find you did not get a perfect fit. You cut the material a bit too short here and there. Do not despair! A number of courses are available to you.

If you have only cut it a little short, you can run a bead of silicone bathtub-caulking compound around the perimeter of the room. Squeeze a small bead out along the bottom of the baseboard. Force it in with your finger and then wash away the excess with a wet rag. This will hide your mistakes and will make your installation truly watertight. This process is in fact recommended by many installers even if there have been no mistakes. Various colored caulking compounds are available to match different colored baseboards.

If you have made a really bad cut, you can put the goods back together and run a bead of seam-sealing compound over the resulting seam. If you have cut inlaid too long and it is too stiff to trim the excess off, heat it carefully with a hair dryer until it is pliable enough to trim.

You may be able to make life a lot easier for yourself right from the beginning by removing your baseboards or by not putting them on, if involved in new construction, until the linoleum has been installed. This provides the width of the baseboard as a margin for error in trimming the material. If you are installing a kitchen or bath including new counters or toilet, leave the counters and toilet out until the floor has been installed. In a bathroom, the toilet should be removed before installing the linoleum anyway, if at all possible.

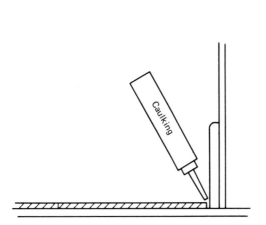

**Fig. 10-19** Squirt caulking into space between linoleum and baseboard.

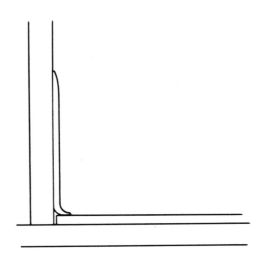

**Fig. 10-20** Cove base can help cover a multitude of trimming sins.

This eliminates the need for a seam behind the toilet and cutting around the toilet. A trimmed edge around the toilet allows moisture from condensation to get under the edge of the linoleum and causes it to curl over the years. Removing the toilet is not essential, but it makes a lot of sense.

Another great assist in trimming linoleum is the use of vinyl or rubber "cove base" (see Fig. 10-20). This can be applied around the perimeter of the room and under counters, in front of shower stalls, even along the front of bathtubs. It is available in many colors. Cove base gives you a nice margin for error (up to ½ of an inch) to work with. It is usually available 2 inches or 4 inches high, and a few colors are 6 inches high. It is relatively inexpensive and very easy to install. Spread adhesive on the back of the base (unless it already is adhesive backed) and press it to the wall or other surface to be covered. Inside and outside corners are available. The material cuts very easily and is available either in 4-foot lengths (most common) or in rolls. Just figure out how much you need, including how many inside and outside corners, purchase it from your floor covering dealer, bring it home, and stick it on.

## REPAIRS

Always save any significant pieces of linoleum that are left over after the initial installation. You may need them to make repairs later on.

Cigarette burns and small tears in linoleum are often a source of aggravation in otherwise perfect installations. This is where most rotogravure products really outshine the inlaids, which can be difficult to repair adequately. Rotogravures are very easy to repair, and often the repair is virtually invisible.

### Rotogravure

Locate a leftover piece of linoleum that exactly duplicates the pattern surrounding the spot that is damaged. You can do this by placing the loose piece on the floor and moving it around until you have gotten all lines in the pattern to match. Having identified the portion of the repair piece you are going to work with, cut out a sufficient amount (perhaps 4 or 6 inches square) to cover the area requiring replacement. This piece can be as little or as large as you deem necessary, but don't make it so small that it is impossible to work with or so large that the following steps become burdensome. One thing to keep in mind is that you will want to cut out your patch (once you start the actual replacement process) following definite lines (such as grout lines) in the pattern.

Once you have this piece in hand, peel the back away from its pattern and wear layer. This will leave you with a relatively thin sheet of vinyl. Now, using masking tape around the edges, tape this sheet to the floor so that it covers the burn and exactly matches the pattern on the floor. Next, cut through both the new piece and the floor underneath around the burn. Cut in short, straight strokes and follow a grout line or other straight line in the pattern as closely as possible. This will make your repair less visible than if you just cut out a circle. Now remove your patch and set it aside. Work the point of your knife gently under the cut you have just made in the floor and peel the wear layer and pattern off, leaving just the back still cemented to the floor. Now apply a thin coat of white household glue to the exposed back. Put your new piece in place, being careful to match the pattern. The last step is to weld the seam exactly as you would the seam in an original installation.

## Inlaid

The same basic system works for inlaid linoleum, except that here you have to work with the entire stiff thickness of the material, not just a thin wear layer over printed pattern. It is helpful to heat the material (with a hair dryer or even an iron—be careful not to burn the floor) to soften it up for easier working. It can be very difficult to double cut an inlaid patch, and you may end up having to create your patch freehand. If possible, experiment with some pieces before attempting the actual repair. Different inlaid linoleums behave in different ways. Yours might be very easy to work with. Once you have set your new patch in place, heat it at the seams until the old and new soften sufficiently for you to work the edges together a bit to help hide the fact that you have made a patch.

# 11  Installing Tile

## LAYING THE FIELD

The first step in installing tile of any type (carpet, vinyl asbestos, asphalt, solid vinyl, or linoleum) is to plan the layout of the tile. Two factors are important. First, make the trimming as easy as possible. Second, lay it out so that it will look all right when finished.

To lay the tile out initially, put it down loose (with no adhesive). It is not necessary to put down the entire floor. In a rectangular room, one strip of tile across the width of the room and another across its length with an intersection in the middle will do. If the room is irregular in shape, a few extra rows may be necessary at strategic points to be sure you have figured things correctly.

To be sure the tile will look all right, make certain the entire pattern is centered and that it runs square to the room—not off at a disturbing angle. Even if the tile has no pattern the lines between the tiles (seams) should run straight and parallel to the walls, and the tiles should be centered. If the walls of the room are way out of square, a compromise will have to be struck— probably lining up the tiles on the straightest and longest wall.

To keep the trimming as easy as possible you can remove the baseboards or use cove base (see Chapter 10). Keep the size of the pieces to be trim- med as large as possible. Some tiles are easier to work with than others. It is best if pieces to be cut off tiles are at least 2 or 3 inches wide. When trimmings get down to 1 inch or less the job becomes very fussy. Also, the field should be centered in the room so that the amount of trim will be approximately equal and slightly less than one-half of a tile all around the room. The field is all of the tiles which can be placed without trim- ming. This way the trimmed halves of the tiles can be used at other parts of the perimeter.

Once you have the layout determined, mark on the subfloor where the first tile is going to be placed. Use a marker that will show through the adhesive you are using. A black indelible pen, for instance, shows through white latex all-purpose adhesive. If you are using a "cut-back" adhesive which must be spread over the entire room and allowed to dry before putting down the tile, the first tile should be marked and placed near the doorway where you can get at it without walking on adhesive.

Unless you are installing self-sticking tiles, your next step is to spread the adhesive. Follow the directions on the container regarding the type of trowel and amount to be spread. Never spread too much, or it may seep up through the seams later on. (See Chapter 8 for cement-spreading tech- niques.) Some adhesives allow you to spread a little

**Fig. 11-1** Loose lay tiles down and across center of room and into irregular shapes to be sure tile will line up the way you want it.

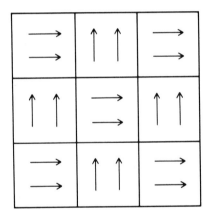

**Fig. 11-2** Pattern or grain in tile is indicated by arrows. Each tile is usually placed at a 90-degree angle to neighboring tiles.

at a time and immediately place the tile. Others require spreading the entire room and letting it dry until it becomes tacky.

Once you have the cement spread to the extent called for you can start placing your tiles. Always do the field first. Normally this goes rather quickly.

*Caution:* Be sure your tiles have been indoors long enough to be at room temperature. Also, do not remove the protective backing from peel-and-stick tiles until you are ready to put the tile in place.

Tiles are usually placed at 90-degree angles to each other. Marbleized tile looks better when the

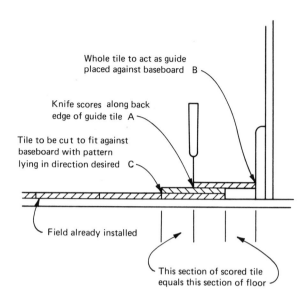

**Fig. 11-3** Scribing tiles to be trimmed as described in numbers 1 to 4 under *Measuring for Trim.*

tiles are not placed with the "grain" all running in the same direction. If you are using more than one box of tile, you should work out of more than one box at a time. There may be a difference in dye lot from one box to another. If you mix up the boxes as you go along you will also mix up the dye lots. If you don't do this, a noticeable difference in shade may show up where you start a new box.

## TRIMMING TILE IN

### Measuring for Trim

The basic technique described here for measuring how much of each tile should be trimmed can be used on all types of tile. Carpet tiles, however, can be trimmed in the same manner as foam-backed carpet (see Chapter 8).

This method can be used only on relatively straight walls which are reasonably parallel to the edges of the field that is already installed. Here's how it works:

1. Place the tile to be cut on top of the piece of field tile it will end up next to. Face its pattern in the correct direction. Line up its edges exactly with the edges of the tile underneath (see Fig. 11-3C).

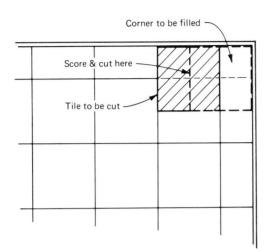

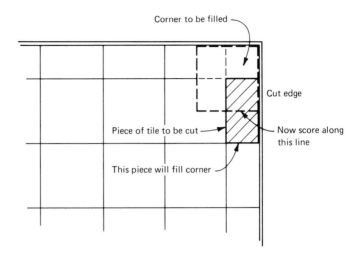

**Fig. 11-4a** For scribing corners (No. 5 in text) shaded area equals tile to be scribed. Dotted line indicates guide tile placed into corner. Score and cut along line shown by arrow.

**Fig. 11-4b** Second stage in scribing corners as described in No. 5.

2. Place another whole tile on top of the tile to be cut but with one edge against the baseboard against which the second tile will ultimately fit. With your utility knife use the back edge of the top tile as a guide and score the tile to be cut.

3. Cut the tile along this line. The piece farthest from the wall will drop into place with its backmost edge against the field and its cut edge against the baseboard.

4. Move along in this manner until you come to a corner. Do not try to trim-in the corner. Go to the next wall and fill all that trim. Do the corners last.

5. Use the same technique for figuring corners. Place a whole tile on one of the half tiles you have just installed adjacent to the corner, lining up its front and back edges with the factory edges of the half tile. Place a whole tile on top with its corner in the corner of the room to be filled and its front edge against the opposite baseboard. Score the tile underneath using the back edge of the guide tile, and cut along this line. Next, move the tile to be cut over to the other half tile, butting the corner to be filled. Keep the edges of the tile you just moved facing in the same direction so that the line you have just cut remains parallel to the wall it must fit against. Follow the same procedure to score a line 90 degrees to the first line you scored. When you finish cutting along these two lines you will end up with a corner piece that fits exactly.

6. For more complicated sections along walls, you can use the scribing techniques described in Chapter 10.

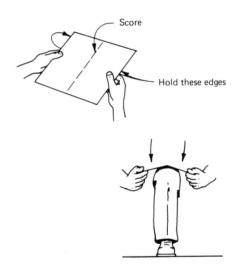

**Fig. 11-5** Vinyl asbestos tile can be cut by scoring with utility knife and then breaking over your leg.

## Cutting Tile

Carpet tiles and soft linoleums and vinyl tiles can be cut with a utility knife as easily as some of the softer linoleums. But the brittle vinyl asbestos and asphalt tiles require a different technique. These can be snapped over your leg. Score the tile several times with the utility knife. Hold the tile with both hands by the edges parallel to the score and break it over your thigh. The tile will break along the scored line.

If the lines are not straight, you have to heat the material in order to cut it (some of the very stiff vinyls may require this too). Once the tiles are heated they soften up enough to cut as you would linoleum. Special blow guns are available for this purpose. Some of the hand-held hair blow dryers may work also. A blowtorch or stove burner can be used. Do not use too much heat, or the tile can melt out of shape or even burn (though it is not likely to burst into flames).

Some tile manufacturers (especially of the self-sticking tiles) suggest using scissors for cutting tile. This can be done, though the material may crumble owing to the action of the scissor blades, unless it has been warmed to make it flexible. Try it out and see which method works best for you.

# 12 Maintenance

To keep your new floor looking good you must keep it clean. This is true of any floor—carpet, linoleum, or tile. The more you let dirt build up on your new floor, the more difficult it will be to bring its original appearance back. Also, an accumulation of dirt and grit can shorten the life of both carpet yarns and linoleum and tile wear layers. The secret, therefore, is to develop a regular maintenance program and to be ready for little emergencies which might arise.

## MAINTAINING YOUR CARPET

### Vacuuming

Carpet should be vacuumed regularly. Different households have different amounts of traffic and different intervals between vacuumings are called for. You probably should vacuum your carpet at least once a week, and you should use the right kind of vacuum. The best kind is one which has powerful suction coupled with a high-speed "beater bar" (see Fig. 12-1). Most upright vacuum cleaners have a beater bar. Many canister types do too. The canister types have two motors—one in the canister creates the suction, and one in the head drives the beater.

The beater-bar action is important because it agitates the strands of yarn and, especially in a deep-pile carpet, brings grit to the surface so it can be drawn off by suction. It also sweeps lint off the surface so it can be drawn away by suction.

Do not be fooled by so-called "electric brooms." These are totally inadequate for the task. They are exactly what they are called. Most have poor suction and no beater bar. They are all right for sweeping smooth surfaces such as linoleum, but that's about it.

A canister vacuum cleaner with no beater bar is better than an electric broom because it probably has better suction, but the beater bar is essential for thorough vacuuming of carpet. If you already have a canister with no beater bar, consider getting a beater bar to go with your present vacuum. If this is not possible, consider purchasing an upright vacuum with no additional attachments (since your canister vacuum probably has all the accessories you need for everything but vacuuming the carpet). Uprights are reasonably priced if you buy the basic machine minus all the frills.

### Spot Cleaning

The secret to getting spots out of carpet is to be prepared to deal with them quickly, before liquids have had a chance to dry.

If you spill coffee, wine, or any other liquid on your carpet, do not panic. Dampen a large sponge and place it over the spill. Press down and let the

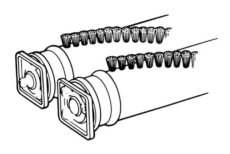

**Fig. 12-1** A vacuum with a beater bar as shown is essential to proper vacuuming of carpet.

liquid come up into the sponge. Squeeze it out in the sink, rinse the sponge and squeeze it out, then press into the spill again. Keep this up until you have gotten out as much as you can. Rinse the sponge again. Then take a glass of cold water (hot may cause alien colors to dye the carpet) and pour the clean water onto the spill. Now repeat the sponging procedure until all the alien color has come out. When you finish your carpet will be wet, but it should dry with no stain. This works even with urine, as long as you get at it quickly—before it dries.

If you can possibly help it, do not rub the carpet. You'll only rub the substance into the nap, making it more difficult to get out.

Some substances are more difficult to deal with than plain liquids, for example raw eggs, vomit, etc. After removing the basic substance as best you can, you may have to do a certain amount of scrubbing. For these emergencies, have handy some carpet detergent (such as Blue Lustre) or mild dishwashing detergent. There are many available. Mix a weak solution of detergent. Pour it over the spot and go to work on it with a soft scrub brush. Scrub gently, or you can destroy the twist in the yarn. After scrubbing, use the sponge procedure to soak out as much as possible. Follow with a rinse of cold water, as described for liquid spills. You may not be able to get all the rinse water out. You will leave your carpet wet. But today's synthetics stand up to moisture. As long as the spot is allowed to dry after cleaning you should have no lasting problem.

Do not use any of these procedures to remove mud. If mud is tracked in let it dry, then vacuum it up. Chances are the carpet will come clean. If there

is a spot left, spray a little all-purpose household cleaner on it, such as Fantastik or Formula 409, and wipe up with a damp sponge. Test such cleaning compounds in a remote area first to be sure the carpet will not be damaged.

Candle wax and chewing gum can be difficult to get out. Try the following. For candle wax, find a blotter (a thick, absorbent paper towel folded several times may work). Place the blotter over the wax. Place an iron on top of the blotter, and heat the iron to the point where the wax melts—be careful not to apply more than about 200 degrees. The wax should melt and soak into the blotter. For chewing gum, put an ice cube into a cloth and place it on the gum. When the gum has frozen, try to break it out of the yarn using a putty knife or other dull instrument.

Many spills besides candle wax and gum are not water soluble. If these occur, find out what the solvent is for the substance involved. Often the label on the container of the spilled substance will tell you. But be very careful. Some solvents can damage the face yarns or the back of the carpet. Run a test in some corner of the carpet where possible damage will not matter before you start attacking a stain right in the middle of the room.

One excellent all-pupose dry cleaner which acts as a solvent for many water-insoluble stains (such as grease) is Renuzit. Do not pour Renuzit onto the carpet. Soak a clean rag with it and then dab or lightly rub the stain. If you allow Renuzit to get down into the back of your carpet, it can dissolve the latex in the back.

No matter what type of stain you are attacking, if you use a white rag or towel you will be able to see if any of the alien color in the stain is coming off onto the rag as you work with it.

**Deep-Down Cleaning**

Perhaps once a year your carpet may become so dirty that regular vacuuming no longer helps. It needs an overall shampooing. Professional rug cleaners can be called in for this purpose. Or you may want to do it yourself. If you do it yourself, here are some suggestions.

Make sure that whatever system you use will show some real results. Be sure that when you have finished you really have cleaned the carpet. Do not be satisfied with a simple "polishing" of the surface

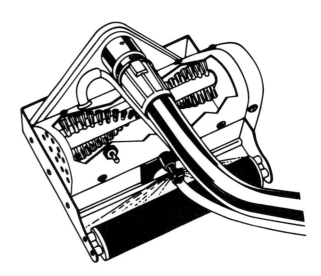

**Fig. 12-2** Carpet cleaning machines, such as RINSEN-VAC shown above, spray carpet with detergent, then remove solution with a powerful wet vacuum. (Courtesy Earl Grissmer Company, Inc.)

**Fig. 12-3** A scrubbing attachment, such as RINSEN-VAC's shown above, will help loosen imbedded dirt prior to extraction. (Courtesy Earl Grissmer Company, Inc.)

which may make the carpet look better momentarily but will not really remove any dirt. When you vacuum, you eventually have to empty the vacuum. When you shampoo the carpet you should expect to have to do the same thing. Yet there are many "systems" on the market today which shampoo the carpet but *take away no dirt.* Where has the dirt gone? The carpet looks better, but no dirt has been removed. The answer is that the dirt still is there. Shampooing has dissolved the dirt on the surface and it has dropped down into the pile. It will come back to the surface soon, and you will be very disappointed within a few days or weeks.

Rent a machine which will show results, not just cleaner looks, but dirt that you have to carry away and dispose of. Rent a machine which truly extracts dirt via a powerful wet vacuum. Many are available today, such as the RINSENVAC® system, a so-called "steam-cleaning" process. Most steam-cleaning systems do not employ steam, but spray the carpet with a hot solution of detergent and immediately extract it with a wet vacuum. The power of the vacuum is the key to the effectiveness of the machine. The more powerful the vacuum, the better the job it can do. A single pass over the carpet with one of these machines may not be enough. It may take several passes before you get the carpet clean.

An even better system than this is one which scrubs the carpet as well as extracts the dirty

detergent solution. This works on much the same principle as a beater bar in a vacuum. Scrubbing agitates the yarns, helping to loosen deep-down dirt. Large "dry foam" scrubber/extractors are available commercially. These put a layer of foam on the carpet, scrub the foam into the nap, and then immediately extract it with a wet vacuum.

For best cleaning, use both processes. Use a scrubber/extractor first, then follow with a rinse using the steam-cleaning system. It is amazing to see how much more dirt comes out with this second process after you think you have gotten the carpet clean with the first. This combination makes for slow going. Therefore, it is difficult to find a commercial cleaner who employs both. Most commercial cleaners either scrub and extract or rinse and extract, rarely both.

Very few dry-foam extraction machines are available to the do-it-yourselfer, so you may have to compromise. Some of the steam-cleaning rental machines do come with a small scrubber built in. The detergent is sprayed into the carpet, a beater-bar brush scrubs the detergent, then the vacuum extracts it. This is a compromise because the scrubber is quite small and cannot possibly do the job the larger scrubbing machines can. For your purposes it might work quite well, but you will have to work harder on really dirty carpet.

A do-it-yourself steam-cleaning machine made by Sears, Roebuck and Co. is now on the market.

While not nearly as powerful as the commercial units, it costs under $200 and may be a worthwhile purchase if you are investing in a lot of wall-to-wall carpet. This machine operates exactly the same as the portable rental steam cleaners. Its major drawback is its relatively low-power wet vacuum. But it is adequate to most tasks, and would be useful in emergencies such as sudden spills and storm damage. Undoubtedly, others will come on the market.

## MAINTAINING YOUR LINOLEUM AND TILE

### Cleaning

Here again, the key to keeping your floor looking nice is to keep it clean. Use a regular maintenance program. Most linoleum and tile floors can be swept or vacuumed quite easily to be sure grit is not left on them for any length of time. If grit is left, it acts as sandpaper that causes the wear layer to wear away.

Spots, of course, can be cleaned much more easily off linoleum than carpet. Just be sure to get all the offending liquid off, leaving no detergent residue.

You also have to wash your floor regularly. Often, especially with the no-wax floors, just using a damp mop is enough. Every now and then, though, you will need to wash the floor thoroughly.

First, be sure you follow washing instructions given by the manufacturer of the floor. This is especially true with regard to the type of detergent you use. Never use a strong detergent; only the mildest type should be employed. If the manufacturer has one, use that.

Second, after washing with detergent rinse thoroughly. This does not mean that you should flood the floor with water. It does mean get rid of any detergent residue. Don't be fooled by labels on household detergents which say you do not need to rinse. This may be all right for walls, but you must rinse your floor. Any detergent residue on the floor will act as a "magnet" and attract dirt. One piece of literature on this subject suggests using two mops for cleaning linoleum. Use one for detergent, one for rinsing. That's how important it is to get all the detergent off the floor.

### Dressings

Some floors, such as asphalt tile, can be waxed with real wax. Waxes are available in both paste and liquid form. These should be applied immediately after the installation of the floor and periodically thereafter depending on how often traffic wears the wax down. Eventually you will get a wax buildup, especially in areas where there is little or no traffic. Then you will have to strip the wax away. This is an arduous task calling for the use of very strong solutions such as ammonia. Many stripping solutions are on the market.

One way to help avoid the buildup and stripping problem is to wax only in areas where the wax really has worn away. Don't apply it in areas where you still get a shine after buffing. Before you decide whether wax is needed be sure the floor really is clean and properly rinsed. A film of dirt and detergent may be your problem—not an absence of wax.

Most floors today do not call for wax. They require special acrylic floor finishes. These are readily available in most floor covering and hardware stores. Also, floor covering manufacturers supply solutions for dressing their floors. If you use the solutions they recommend you can be confident of good results. Avoid the buildup and stripping problem by only reapplying acrylic finish where the floor has lost its shine. Here again, be sure dullness is not the result of detergent or dirt buildup.

## NO-WAX FLOOR MAINTENANCE

A floor that has a factory-applied wear layer of polyurethane should require no dressing for several years. Regular cleaning should keep it shiny. But once the finish dulls in high-traffic areas, you will need to purchase the finish made specifically for this purpose by the manufacturer of the floor. Apply it only in areas where the floor has dulled and become more difficult to clean—not all over. Otherwise you will get a buildup problem that may cause yellowing.

Finally, floors with a clear polyvinyl chloride (PVC) wear layer may be maintained two ways. One is to apply a dressing as called for by the manufacturer. A second way is suggested by GAF Congoleum and Mannington. Buff the floor with a lamb's wool pad. This process may eliminate dullness by removing film you have not been able to get rid of and by "recuring" the PVC wear layer with friction. You can rent a buffing machine at almost any home-product store or power tool rental outlet. Be sure the floor is clean and dry before buffing.

Of course, buffing does not protect the wear layer with another layer of dressing. Continual buffing will wear the PVC away slowly but surely. If you apply a dressing it will protect the surface of the vinyl. The thinner the wear layer, the more important it may be to apply a dressing.

# 13 Metal Edgings

The number of metal trims which can be used for finishing off the exposed edges of floor covering (carpet, linoleum, and tile) is practically endless. I will not, therefore, attempt to describe every kind available on the market today, but only the basic types used by most installers.

There are two basic types of metal trims—those which must be installed after the new floor and those which must be installed before the new floor.

The first kind is most readily available in most hardware and building-supply stores. These are anodized aluminum strips (silver and gold) usually 3 or 6 feet long and ½ of an inch or more wide. Some are flat, some have an offset angle, and some are curved (see Fig. 13-1). The different shapes enable the installer to finish the edges of very thick or very thin floor covering in relation to various adjacent surfaces ranging from door thresholds to plain wood floors. You have to judge what will work best for you. You may need different types for different situations in the same installation.

The advantage of the door metals you install last is that they are relatively easy to install. They are simply nailed (or screwed) down as a final step in the overall floor-covering installation. And a wide metal strip can be counted on to cover a multitude of trimming problems.

With tackless carpet installation you have to fasten your carpet into the doorway permanently *prior to* applying the metal. One way is to run a strip of tackless across the door, hook the carpet onto the tackless, then fasten the metal in place. Or you can avoid the use of metal entirely by folding the carpet under in the doorway and tacking it in place every 1½ inches.

The second kind of metal trim (installed prior to laying the floor) is usually available only from floor-covering dealers. These door metals are specially designed for the trade. They come in an amazing variety of sizes and shapes, but there are certain basic types designed for particular uses.

1. Clampdown metal with pins. Use this type for tackless carpet installations. Install clampdown metal with pins at the same time you install tackless stripping, along the perimeter of the room (such as doorways) where there is no baseboard against which the carpet can be trimmed. Clampdown metals have "pins" sticking out of them at an angle, like tackless stripping. Stretch the carpet onto these pins as onto tackless, and trim it off immediately behind the edge of the metal. Then tuck it under the edge and bend the edge back (clamped down) over the carpet, binding the carpet onto the pins. Clamp the metal down with a hammer, striking

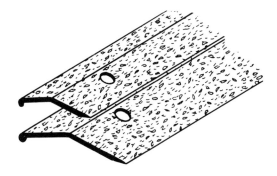

**Fig. 13-1** Metals available as shown by Roberts above would be installed after the floor has been installed. (Courtesy Roberts Consolidated Industries.)

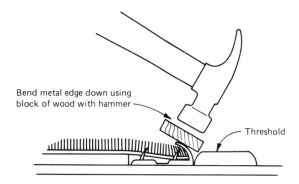

**Fig. 13-3** Carpet is trimmed to just under the edge, hooked onto pins (after stretch). Edge is bent back as shown with hammer.

**Fig. 13-2** Clampdown metals must be installed prior to installing the floor. (Courtesy Roberts Consolidated Industries.)

**Fig. 13-4** Clampdown metal without pins for use with foam-back carpet also is installed prior to flooring. Also can be used with linoleum and tile. (Courtesy Roberts Consolidated Industries)

from above. Use a block of wood or carpet scrap to prevent denting the metal unnecessarily (see Fig. 13-3). When the installation is complete only the edge of the metal is exposed, usually a strip about ½ of an inch wide. Clampdown metal with pins is available with four finishes: gold or silver anodized and smooth or "hammered."

2. Clampdown metal without pins. Use this metal for glue-down installations of either jute-backed or foam-backed carpet. Clampdown metal without pins performs exactly the same function as the kind with pins, and is available with the same finishes. The difference is the section that remains under the carpet is flat, and therefore leaves no bulge under the carpet after it has been installed. You can also use clampdown without pins with linoleum and tile installations, although they leave a wider edge of metal exposed than some of the

more traditional linoleum metals. The wider edge can work to your advantage, as it allows greater margin for error in trimming. For the do-it-yourselfer, this type may be the best for linoleum installations.

3. "Universal" metals with or without pins. Use these as you would the kinds already described. They have an additional plastic strip (available in various colors to match the carpet) which is inserted into a channel after the floor covering has been installed. The plastic strip on universal metal is available with an offset so that the edge can be finished to a surface lower than that of the new floor covering.

4. Linoleum metals. These are similar to clampdown metals without pins except that the exposed edge is very narrow. The width of the edge depends on the thickness of the linoleum to

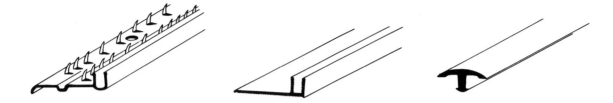

**Fig. 13-5** Universal metals are installed prior to flooring. Vinyl inserts go in after floor has been fitted to metal. (Courtesy Roberts Consolidated Industries)

be installed. The heavier the gauge of the linoleum, the wider the metal edge. Linoleum metals require careful trimming of the linoleum because a net fit to the metal must be achieved to make it look right.

5. Many other kinds of metal trims are available though your dealer may not carry them. Chances are, however, the dealer will have a supplier's catalog from which you can pick what you need.

# Index

common sense, 47, 48

compass, pencil, 87, 88, 89

compete, 19, 26

complain(t), 20, 38, 46

compression seam, 66

concrete, 52, 53, 71, 72

condensation, 53, 94

configuration(s), yarn, 24, 25

"conductive," re: static electricity, 25

Congoleum, 43, 44, 45, 46
    Spring, 45

connoisseur, 30

corrugated cardboard, 79

consumer(s), 19, 20, 24, 26, 38

contact adhesive, 45, 86

contours, 4

controversy, 37, 52

cork, powdered, 43

costs, 19, 20, 24, 26, 47, 48, 49
    do-it-yourself, 48
    labor, 47
    low, 26

cotton, 24, 26, 34, 36

couch, 6, 7, 19

counter(s), 13, 14, 16, 93, 94

counter space, 2, 3

country, 19, 47, 49

cover base, vinyl and rubber, 94, 97

crease, 59, 60, 62, 85

crevices, 56

cross-seam, 16, 17

crumbs, 31

Cumuloft (nylon), 25

cured, 52, 53

curl(s)(ing), 45, 46, 51, 54, 59, 79, 86, 92, 94

cushion, carpet, 36

cushioned linoleum, 22, 45, 48, 51, 53, 83

cushions, 37, 44

customer(s), 20, 39, 48, 51
    unsuspecting, 39

cut(s), bad, 93

cut and loop, 32, 35

cut pile, 28, 29, 30, 32, 33, 34, 35, 38, 54

cut-back adhesive, 97

cutout(s), 4, 8, 57, 61

cutter, tackless, 71

damage:
    linoleum back, 45
    prevention of, 102
    repair of linoleum, 94, 95
    storm, 104

damp cellar, 52

damp mop, 44, 104

dampness, 26

dangerous fumes, 45

dangerous, asbestos dust, 51

dealer(s), 1, 5, 19, 20, 21, 27, 38, 39, 46, 47, 48, 49, 52, 57, 67, 78, 92, 94, 107, 109

decorator, 21

deep pile, 28, 33, 63, 70, 101

defect, 19, 30, 38, 46

deflection (initial load, indent load) 38

delamination, 46

delivery, 19

dense pad, 22, 37

dense weave, 28

density, 26, 27, 28, 37, 38

deposit, 21

design(s), 30, 32, 59

detergent:
    carpet, 102, 103
    dishwashing, 102
    linoleum, 104

deteriorate, 36, 38, 54

developments, recent, 24, 25, 26, 45

diagram(s), 1, 3, 4, 5, 6, 7, 8, 12, 16, 67

dining area, 13

direct glue down, 36, 81, 108

direction:
    carpet, 3, 5
    linoleum, 14
    nap, 6, 7, 8, 9

dirt, 24, 31, 32, 46, 101, 103, 104

disarray, strands of yarn, 30

dishonest practice, 39

dishwashing detergent, 102

disintegrate, 37

disposable trowel, 49

distributor(s), wholesale, 19, 20, 39

do-it-yourself(er), 22, 24, 45, 46, 47, 48, 49, 83, 102, 103, 108

dollar, 19

doormat, 4, 61

door(s)(ways), 1, 3, 4, 5, 12, 13, 14, 16, 47, 48, 49, 56, 57, 58, 59, 60, 61, 71, 72, 80, 83, 86, 88, 97, 107
    frame(s), 58, 59
    jamb, 59, 72, 88
    metal(s), 47, 48, 49, 107
    thresholds, 107
    trim, 59

double cutting, 92, 93

double-faced tape, 60, 61, 64, 86, 92

dowel, 58

drainage, 52

drapes, 22

dress(ed)(ings), 44, 46, 104, 105

dry, buffing linoleum, 44

drive pins, tackless, 72

dry cleaner, 102

dry foam, 103

duct(s), forced hot air, 72, 73

duct tape, 73

dull(s)(ness), 44, 104, 105

durability, 24, 27, 28, 32, 43, 46

durable, 26, 28, 29, 34, 36, 38, 43, 45

dust, 22, 46, 51, 58, 67, 84, 87

dye, 102

dye(d)(ing), solution, 25, 26

dye-lot, 48, 98

easy(ier):
    to clean, 21, 26, 46
    to install, 22, 24, 43, 45, 46, 57, 107
    to maintain, 26, 43, 44

edge(s), 8, 10, 11, 15, 16, 24, 27, 28, 45, 46, 51, 54, 57, 58, 59, 60, 61, 62, 63, 64, 65, 66, 67, 68, 73, 76, 77, 78, 79, 80, 82, 83, 84, 85, 86, 87, 89, 90, 91, 92, 93, 94, 95, 98, 107, 108, 109